Funtastic Math

# Decimals and Fractions

by Cynthia Mitchell

SCHOLASTIC
PROFESSIONAL BOOKS

New York ✳ Toronto ✳ London ✳ Auckland ✳ Sydney

$$3\frac{1}{2} + 8\frac{1}{6} + \frac{1}{8} = ? \qquad \frac{1}{2} = \frac{2}{4} = \frac{4}{8} \qquad 0.5 = 0.50 = 0.500 \qquad 123.456789 + 9876.54321 = ?$$

Edited by Sarah Glasscock

Cover design by Jaime Lucero and Vincent Ceci

Cover Illustration by Michael Moran

Interior design by Ellen Matlach Hassell
for Boultinghouse & Boultinghouse, Inc.

Interior illustrations by Kate Flanagan and Manuel Rivera

ISBN 0-590-37365-X

$$3\tfrac{1}{2} + 8\tfrac{1}{6} + \tfrac{1}{8} = ? \quad * \quad \tfrac{1}{2} = \tfrac{2}{4} = \tfrac{4}{8} \quad * \quad 0.5 = 0.50 = 0.500 \quad * \quad 123.456789 + 9876.54321 = ?$$

# Contents

Introduction . . . . . . . . . . . . . . . . . . . . . . . . . . . . . . . .5
National Council of Teachers of Mathematics Standards . . . . . . . . . . . . .7

## FRACTIONS

### Equivalent Fractions

* The Mysterious Fraction Zone . . . . . . . . . . . . . . . . . . . . . .8
Fraction Snowflakes . . . . . . . . . . . . . . . . . . . . . . . . . . .10

### Lowest Terms and LCD

* The Wheel of Fractions . . . . . . . . . . . . . . . . . . . . . . . .11
* Optical Illusions . . . . . . . . . . . . . . . . . . . . . . . . . . .13

### Comparing and Ordering Fractions

* Sensational Surveys . . . . . . . . . . . . . . . . . . . . . . . . . .15
Fraction Line-Up . . . . . . . . . . . . . . . . . . . . . . . . . . . .17

### Mixed Numbers

Shoot for the Stars . . . . . . . . . . . . . . . . . . . . . . . . . . .18
The Great Fraction Race . . . . . . . . . . . . . . . . . . . . . . . . .19

### Addition and Subtraction of Like Fractions

* Four in a Row Fractions . . . . . . . . . . . . . . . . . . . . . . . .20
Shout It Out! . . . . . . . . . . . . . . . . . . . . . . . . . . . . . .22

### Addition and Subtraction of Unlike Fractions

* Teacher Troubles . . . . . . . . . . . . . . . . . . . . . . . . . . .24
Fraction Trios . . . . . . . . . . . . . . . . . . . . . . . . . . . . .26

### Multiplication and Division

* Tangram Fractions . . . . . . . . . . . . . . . . . . . . . . . . . . .27
* Ladybug Fractions . . . . . . . . . . . . . . . . . . . . . . . . . . .29
Don't Let Fractions Drive You Buggy . . . . . . . . . . . . . . . . . . .31

### Relating Fractions with Mixed Numbers and Decimals

* Clowning Around . . . . . . . . . . . . . . . . . . . . . . . . . . . .32
Battling Decimals . . . . . . . . . . . . . . . . . . . . . . . . . . . .34

*(continued on the next page)*

* Activity includes a student reproducible.

# DECIMALS

## Reading and Writing Decimals

✳ Stumpers . . . . . . . . . . . . . . . . . . . . . . . . . . . . . . . . . . .35

Name That Decimal . . . . . . . . . . . . . . . . . . . . . . . . . . . . .37

## Place Value

Guess That Decimal . . . . . . . . . . . . . . . . . . . . . . . . . . . . .38

✳ Every Number Has Its Place . . . . . . . . . . . . . . . . . . . . . . .39

## Comparing and Ordering Decimals

✳ "Weighty" Problems . . . . . . . . . . . . . . . . . . . . . . . . . . . .41

✳ Wacky Presidential Firsts . . . . . . . . . . . . . . . . . . . . . . . . .43

Who's First? . . . . . . . . . . . . . . . . . . . . . . . . . . . . . . . . . .45

## Rounding Decimals

✳ Decimal Roundup . . . . . . . . . . . . . . . . . . . . . . . . . . . . . .46

Top Secret Numbers . . . . . . . . . . . . . . . . . . . . . . . . . . . . .48

## Equivalent Decimals

Bag Math . . . . . . . . . . . . . . . . . . . . . . . . . . . . . . . . . . . .49

Guarded Treasure . . . . . . . . . . . . . . . . . . . . . . . . . . . . . . .50

## Addition and Subtraction

✳ Absolutely Magical . . . . . . . . . . . . . . . . . . . . . . . . . . . . .51

✳ Shopping in the "Good Old Days . . . . . . . . . . . . . . . . . . . .53

✳ Running for the Gold . . . . . . . . . . . . . . . . . . . . . . . . . . . .55

## Multiplication and Division

✳ Decimal Points Everywhere . . . . . . . . . . . . . . . . . . . . . . . .57

Decimal Puzzlers . . . . . . . . . . . . . . . . . . . . . . . . . . . . . . .59


Do I Have Problems! . . . . . . . . . . . . . . . . . . . . . . . . . . . . .60

Student Self-Evaluation . . . . . . . . . . . . . . . . . . . . . . . . . . .63

Teacher Assessment Form . . . . . . . . . . . . . . . . . . . . . . . . . .64

✳ Activity includes a student reproducible.

# Introduction

With this book of activities, part of a six-book mathematics series, we hope to make teaching and understanding fractions and decimals fun, creative, and exciting.

## An Overview of the Book

### Table of Contents

The table of contents features the activity names and page numbers, as well as stars to mark student reproducibles. Activities are categorized by fraction or decimal topic, so you may use the table of contents as a scope and sequence.

## Teaching Pages

Everything you need to know is on the teaching page, but you also have the option of tailoring the activities to meet students' individual needs and to address the wide variety of skills displayed in your classroom.

### Learning Logo

A logo indicating the fraction or decimal topic being discussed appears at the top of the page. The logo is correlated to the topics in the table of contents. This will enable you to key the activities to your mathematics curriculum quickly and easily.

### Learning Objective

The objective clearly states the primary aim of the activity.

### Grouping

This states whether the whole class, individual students, pairs, or cooperative groups should perform the task. If an activity lends itself to more than one grouping, the choices are indicated. Again, if you feel that another grouping is more appropriate to your classroom, feel free to alter the activity accordingly.

### Materials

To cut your preparation time, all materials necessary for the main activity (including student reproducible) and its extension are listed. Most of the materials are probably already in your classroom. If an activity has a student reproducible with it, the page number of the reproducible is listed here.

### Advance Preparation

A few activities require some minimal advance preparation on your part. All the directions you need are given here. You may also let students take over some or all of the preparation.

### Directions

The directions usually begin with suggestions on how to introduce or review the fraction or decimal topic, including any terms and/or formulas. Step-by-step details on how to do the activity follow. When pertinent, specific strategies that might help students in solving problems are suggested.

### Taking It Farther

This section on the teaching page offers suggestions on how you can extend and enrich the activity. Students who require extra help and those who need a challenge will both benefit when you move the activity to a different level.

### Assessing Skills

The key questions and/or common errors pointed out in this section will help alert you to students' progress. (In fact, you may want to jot down more questions on the page.) Use the information you gather about students here in conjunction with the teacher assessment form that appears on page 64 of the book.

### Answers

When answers are called for, they appear on the teaching page.

## Student Reproducibles

About one-third of the activities have a companion student reproducible page for you to duplicate and distribute. These activities are marked with a star in the table of contents.

## Do I Have Problems!

These pages are filled with fun and challenging Problems of the Day that you may write on the board or post on the bulletin board. The answers appear in brackets at the end of each problem.

## Assessment

### Student Self-Evaluation Form

At the end of the activity, hand out these forms for students to complete. Emphasize that their responses are for themselves as well as you. Evaluating their own performances will help students clarify their thinking and understand more about their reasoning.

### Teacher Assessment Form and Scoring Rubric

The sign of a student's success with an activity is more than a correct answer. As the NCTM stresses, problem solving, communication, reasoning, and connections are equally important in the mathematical process. How a student arrives at the answer—the strategies she or he uses or discards, for instance—can be as important as the answer itself. This assessment form and scoring rubric will help you determine the full range of students' mastery of skills.

# National Council of Teachers of Mathematics Standards

The activities in this book, and the rest of the series, have been written with the National Council of Teachers of Mathematics (NCTM) Standards in mind. The first four standards—Mathematics as Problem Solving, Mathematics as Communication, Mathematics as Reasoning, and Mathematical Connections—form the philosophical underpinning of the activities.

## Standard 1: Mathematics as Problem Solving
The open-ended structure of the activities, and their extension, builds and strengthens students' problem-solving skills.

## Standard 2: Mathematics as Communication
Class discussion at the beginning and ending of the activities is an integral part of these activities.

Additionally, communication is fostered when students work in pairs or cooperative groups and when individuals share and compare work.

## Standard 3: Mathematics as Reasoning
Communicating their processes in working these activities gives students the opportunity to understand and appreciate their own thinking.

## Standard 4: Mathematical Connections
A variety of situations has been incorporated into the activities to give students a broad base on which to apply mathematics. Topics range from real-life experiences (historical and contemporary) to the whimsical and fantastic, so students can expand their mathematical thinking to include other subject areas.

---

**More specifically, the activities in this book address the following NCTM Standards.**

## Grades K–4:

### Standard 5: Estimation
* Explore estimation strategies.
* Recognize when an estimate is appropriate.
* Determine the reasonableness of results.
* Apply estimation in working with quantities, measurement, computation, and problem solving.

### Standard 6: Number Sense and Numeration
* Construct number meanings through real-world experiences and the use of physical materials.
* Understand our numeration system by relating counting, grouping, and place-value concepts.
* Develop number sense.
* Interpret the multiple uses of numbers encountered in the real world.

### Standard 12: Fractions and Decimals
* Develop concepts of fractions, mixed numbers, and decimals.
* Develop number sense for fractions and decimals.
* Use models to relate fractions to decimals and to find equivalent fractions.
* Use models to explore operations on fractions and decimals.
* Apply fractions and decimals to problem situations.

## Grades 5–8:

### Standard 5: Number and Number Relationships
* Understand, represent, and use numbers in a variety of equivalent forms (integer, fraction, decimal, percent, exponential, and scientific notation) in real-world and mathematical problem situations.
* Develop number sense for whole numbers, fractions, decimals, integers, and rational numbers.

### Standard 6: Number Systems and Number Theory
* Develop and order relations for whole numbers, fractions, decimals, integers, and rational numbers.
* Understand how the basic arithmetic operations are related to each other.
* Develop and apply number theory concepts (e.g., primes, factors, and multiples) in real-world and mathematical problem situations.

### Standard 7: Computation and Estimation
* Compute with whole numbers, fractions, decimals, integers, and rational numbers.
* Develop, analyze, and explain procedures for computation and techniques for estimation.
* Select and use an appropriate method for computing from among mental arithmetic, paper-and-pencil, calculator, and computer methods.
* Use computation, estimation, and proportions to solve problems.
* Use estimation to check the reasonableness of results.

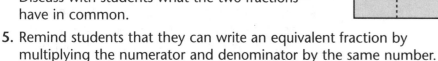

$3\frac{1}{2} + 8\frac{1}{6} + \frac{1}{8} = ?$ ✳ $\frac{1}{2} = \frac{2}{4} = \frac{4}{8}$ ✳ $0.5 = 0.50 = 0.500$ ✳ $123.45$

**Equivalent Fractions**

# The Mysterious Fraction Zone

**What do learning about equivalent fractions and investigating the Bermuda Triangle have in common? Fun and intrigue!**

## ⟳→ Directions

1. Duplicate *The Mysterious Fraction Zone* reproducible for each student.

2. Review the term *equivalent fractions*. Remind students that equivalent fractions have the same value, such as $\frac{1}{3}$ and $\frac{2}{6}$.

3. Fold a piece of paper in half and shade one half lightly with a marker. Ask a volunteer to tell what fraction represents the shaded area. [$\frac{1}{2}$]

4. Fold another piece of paper in half, and then in half again, to create fourths. Shade two sections, $\frac{2}{4}$, lightly with a marker. Ask a volunteer to tell what fraction represents the shaded area. [$\frac{2}{4}$] Discuss with students what the two fractions have in common.

5. Remind students that they can write an equivalent fraction by multiplying the numerator and denominator by the same number.

6. To rename a fraction that is not in lowest terms, they can find the greatest common factor and then divide the numerator and denominator by it.

## ☆ Taking It Farther

Encourage students to find more facts about the Bermuda Triangle or other unsolved mysteries. They can write their own equivalent fractions to match the facts.

## ✓ Assessing Skills

✳ Observe whether students are taking the original fraction and multiplying the numerator and denominator randomly to find equivalent fractions, or if they are dividing the numerator and denominator to rename the fraction in lowest terms.

✳ If students are dividing the numerator and denominator to reduce fractions to lowest terms, are they randomly dividing or using the greatest common factor?

### LEARNING OBJECTIVE

Students find equivalent fractions.

### GROUPING

Individual

### MATERIALS

✳ 2 pieces of paper

✳ markers

For each student:

✳ *The Mysterious Fraction Zone* reproducible (p. 9)

✳ paper and pencil

### ANSWERS

*Mary Celeste* $\frac{1}{3}$ ($\frac{10}{30}$, $\frac{3}{9}$)

Avengers $\frac{4}{5}$ ($\frac{8}{10}$, $\frac{40}{50}$)

Atlantis $\frac{1}{2}$ ($\frac{50}{100}$, $\frac{6}{12}$)

USS *Cyclops* $\frac{2}{7}$ ($\frac{6}{21}$, $\frac{4}{14}$)

# The Mysterious Fraction Zone

Welcome to the Mysterious Fraction Zone—where every fraction is equivalent to an unexplained mystery!

Hundreds of planes and ships have vanished without a trace in an area of the Atlantic Ocean known as the Bermuda Triangle. Pilots have reported spinning compasses, loss of electric power, and jammed equipment.

Some people think the triangle has unusual magnetic or gravitational forces. Others conclude that the disappearances are due to weather, pilot error, or other explainable conditions. Decide for yourself.

## WHAT TO DO:
❋ **Match the fraction under each picture to the two equivalent fractions in the Fact Bank. These facts reveal a mystery.**

❋ **Write the equivalent fractions and mystery facts on a separate sheet of paper. The order of the facts isn't important.**

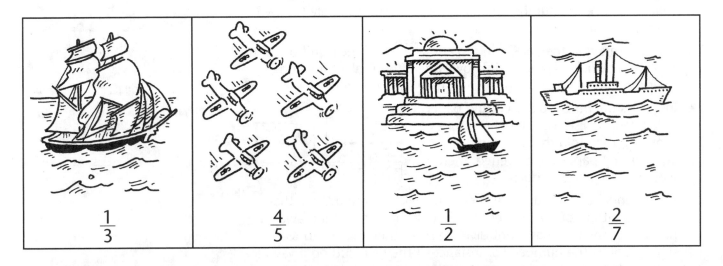

$\frac{1}{3}$     $\frac{4}{5}$     $\frac{1}{2}$     $\frac{2}{7}$

# FACT BANK

$\frac{50}{100}$ In 335 B.C. Plato wrote about an ancient empire, Atlantis, that after a day and night of rain sank to the bottom of the ocean.

$\frac{8}{10}$ Five Avenger torpedo bombers in perfect working order left Fort Lauderdale Naval Air Station with full loads of fuel on a clear day.

$\frac{6}{12}$ Underwater expeditions in the Bermuda Triangle have uncovered stone heads, carved pillars, and pyramids believed to be part of the lost civilization of Atlantis.

$\frac{6}{21}$ The USS *Cyclops*, a 19,600-ton Navy boat, left the West Indies bound for Norfolk, Virginia, but it never arrived.

$\frac{40}{50}$ Several hours after takeoff, the Avengers radioed the control tower, saying that everything was strange and they were not sure of their directions . . . then, silence.

$\frac{10}{30}$ The *Mary Celeste*, a 103-foot-long ship, was found perfectly intact and abandoned at sea. There was no sign of bad weather or foul play.

$\frac{4}{14}$ The navy boat—and its 309 crew members— disappeared without a trace in fair weather, without sending an SOS.

$\frac{3}{9}$ What mysterious event would lead Captain Briggs, his wife, his daughter, and eight crew members to leave their ship with a meal still on the table?

 $3\frac{1}{2} + 8\frac{1}{6} + \frac{1}{8} = ?$ ✳ $\frac{1}{2} = \frac{2}{4} = \frac{4}{8}$ ✳ $0.5 = 0.50 = 0.500$ ✳ $123.45$

**Equivalent Fractions**

# Fraction Snowflakes

**Students create a whole roomful of unique snowflakes while exploring equivalent fractions.**

## ⟶ Directions

1. Review finding a missing numerator in equivalent fractions. Write the example below on the board. Remind students that 4 is multiplied by 25 to get 100, so the 1 must be multiplied by 25 to get 25.

$$\frac{1}{4} = \frac{n}{100} \qquad \frac{1 \times 25}{4 \times 25} = \frac{25}{100}$$

2. Have students find the number of squares on their grid paper without counting every square. They can count the number of squares down, the number of squares across, and multiply the two to find the total number of squares.

3. Tell students that they are going to cut away $\frac{1}{4}$ of their grid paper to make a snowflake. Using their knowledge of equivalent fractions, they can find the number of squares they should cut away.

4. Instruct students to fold their grid paper in half lengthwise with the grid squares showing, then fold the paper in half again. If the paper were opened, there would be four equal squares.

5. As students begin cutting out their snowflakes, remind them that they are cutting out 4 squares at a time. If they are cutting away a number of squares that is not divisible by 4, they may need to slightly adjust the number. For instance, if they are cutting away 25 squares, they would adjust the number to 24, which is easily divisible by 4. Therefore, they would cut away 6 squares.

6. Remind students to take care when cutting along the sides that are fold lines. If they cut down both fold lines, the paper will be cut into four separate pieces.

7. Attach yarn to the snowflakes and display them around the classroom.

## ★ Taking It Farther

Encourage students to make snowflakes with $\frac{1}{2}$ or $\frac{3}{4}$ of the squares cut away. Discuss which snowflakes are the easiest to make and which are the most intricate.

## ✓ Assessing Skills

Are students able to apply their knowledge of equivalent fractions and find the number of squares they need to eliminate?

### LEARNING OBJECTIVE

Given a fraction, students find equivalent fractions.

### GROUPING

Individual

### MATERIALS

For each student:

✳ scissors

✳ sheet of grid paper

✳ yarn

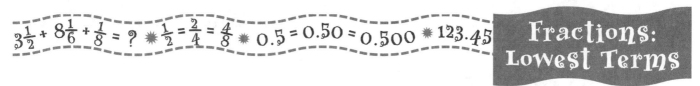
# The Wheel of Fractions

**Renaming fractions in this easy-to-assemble game spells nothing but fun!**

## ⟳→ Directions

1. Duplicate the reproducible for each pair.

2. To make the Wheel of Fractions, students cut out the Wheel of Fraction game pieces. They also cut out the window and window flap as directed. Then they place Figure 1 on top of Figure 2, punch a hole in the middle of both figures, put the paper fastener into the hole, and spread the tabs flat. **Tip:** To make the wheel easier to spin and the game longer lasting, laminate it, print it on oak tag, or glue the printed page to paper plates.

3. Students decide who will go first. In turn, a player spins the Wheel of Fractions with the spinner tab and reads the fraction in the window.

4. The player renames the fraction in lowest terms and opens the answer flap to see if the answer is correct.

5. If the answer is correct, that player collects the amount of money shown in the window. If the answer is incorrect, no money is collected. Then the next player takes a turn.

6. The first player to earn $100 wins the game.

## ☆ Taking It Farther

Encourage students to make their own Wheel of Fraction games. They can trace the circle in Figure 2 and write questions and answers. Some topic suggestions include changing improper fractions to mixed numbers, changing fractions to decimals, or finding a missing number in equivalent fractions.

## ✓ Assessing Skills

Are students using the greatest common factor to rename the fraction, or repeated division?

### LEARNING OBJECTIVE

Students rename fractions in lowest terms.

### GROUPING

Pairs

### MATERIALS

For each pair:

* *Wheel of Fractions* reproducible (p. 12)

* scissors

* 1 brass paper fastener

* play money (up to $200 in ones, fives, tens, and twenties)

* oak tag or paper plates (optional)

# The Wheel of Fractions...

**where renaming fractions spells nothing but fun!**

Figure 1

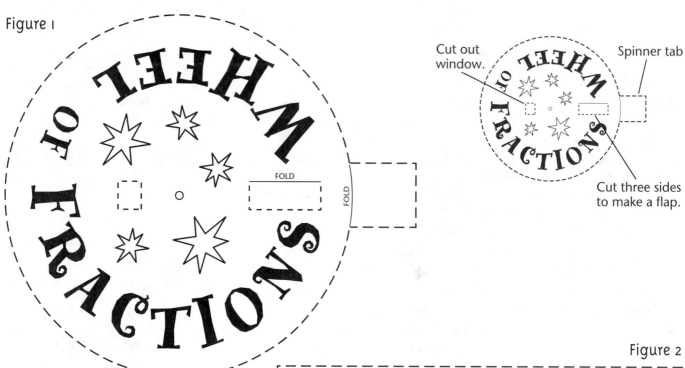

Cut out window.

Spinner tab

Cut three sides to make a flap.

Figure 2

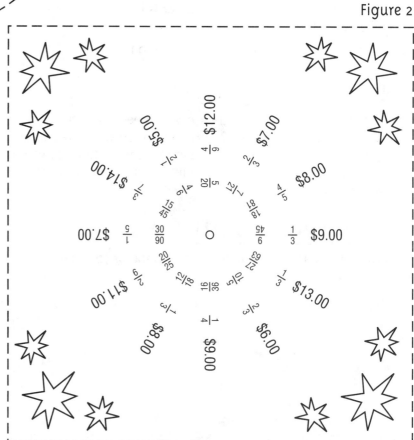

$3\frac{1}{2} + 8\frac{1}{6} + \frac{1}{8} = ?$ ✳ $\frac{1}{2} = \frac{2}{4} = \frac{4}{8}$ ✳ $0.5 = 0.50 = 0.500$ ✳ $123.45$

**Fractions: Lowest Terms**

# Optical Illusions

As fractions are renamed and colored, the flower blossoms and becomes three-dimensional.

## ➤ Directions

1. Duplicate the reproducible for each student.

2. Draw the following lines of equal length on the board:

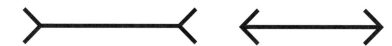

   Ask students which line looks longer. Then have a volunteer measure the length of each line with a ruler.

3. Explain that the two lines are an example of an optical illusion. The line on the left only appears to be longer than the line on the right.

4. Write the following fractions on the board: $\frac{1}{3}$ and $\frac{311}{933}$. Ask students which fraction they believe is larger. Guide them as necessary in determining that the two fractions are equivalent.

5. Allow students to complete the reproducible on their own.

## ☆ Taking It Farther

✳ Direct students to find other fractions that are equivalent to $\frac{1}{2}$, $\frac{1}{3}$, and $\frac{1}{4}$. They may make their own optical illusions for classmates to solve.

✳ After the fractions have been renamed, challenge advanced students to add all of the fractions and find the sum for the reproducible.

✳ Students enjoy solving patterns using the concept of equivalent fractions. Present the following for them to solve:

$$\frac{1}{4}, \frac{3}{12}, \frac{9}{36}, \frac{?}{?}, \frac{?}{?}, \frac{?}{?}$$

$$\frac{304}{416}, \frac{152}{208}, \frac{?}{?}, \frac{?}{?}, \frac{?}{?}$$

## ✓ Assessing Skills

Are students using the greatest common factor or repeated division?

### LEARNING OBJECTIVE

Students rename fractions and find their lowest terms equivalent.

### GROUPING

Individual

### MATERIALS

For each student:

✳ *Optical Illusions* reproducible (p. 14)

✳ ruler

✳ crayons or colored pencils

### ANSWERS

Dark blue:
$\frac{19}{38}, \frac{6}{12}, \frac{7}{14}, \frac{25}{50}, \frac{11}{22}, \frac{50}{100}, \frac{17}{34}, \frac{4}{8}$

Red:
$\frac{7}{21}, \frac{10}{30}, \frac{3}{9}, \frac{4}{12}$

Dark blue:
$\frac{2}{8}, \frac{25}{100}, \frac{10}{40}, \frac{13}{52}, \frac{3}{12}, \frac{4}{16}, \frac{8}{32}, \frac{7}{28}$

# Optical Illusions

Color the fractions equivalent to ½ dark blue. Color the fractions equivalent to ⅓ red. Color the fractions equivalent to ¼ light blue.

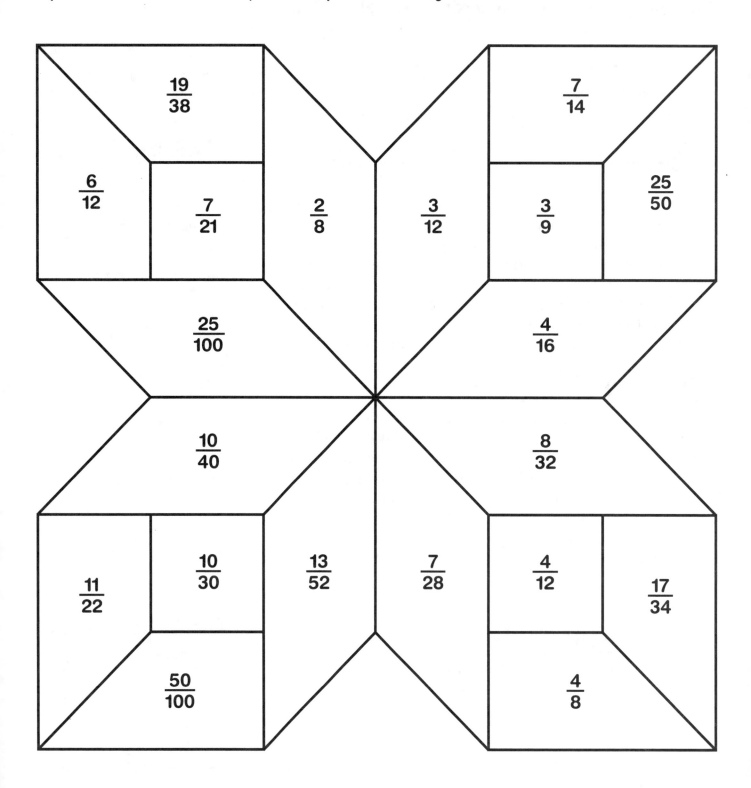

*Decimals and Fractions* Scholastic Professional Books

$3\frac{1}{2} + 8\frac{1}{6} + \frac{1}{8} = ?$ ✹ $\frac{1}{2} = \frac{2}{4} = \frac{4}{8}$ ✹ $0.5 = 0.50 = 0.500$ ✹ $123.45$

**Fractions: Comparing & Ordering**

# Sensational Surveys

**Students work in groups to design a survey, gather information, graph data, and share their results. They see that fractions have real-life applications.**

## ⟳→ Directions

1. Review stating information in fractional form.

   a. Twenty people were asked which pets they liked the best with the following results: cats (5), dogs (10), turtles (1), birds (1), snakes (2), and mice (1).

   b. Here are the data written in fractional form:

   cats ($\frac{5}{20} = \frac{1}{4}$), dogs ($\frac{10}{20} = \frac{1}{2}$), turtles ($\frac{1}{20}$), birds ($\frac{1}{20}$), snakes ($\frac{2}{20} = \frac{1}{10}$), and mice ($\frac{1}{20}$)

2. Review writing data on circle graphs. If you have access to computers with graphing software, familiarize students with this process. If computers are not available, follow the steps below.

   a. Divide a 12-inch cardboard circle into fourths with a light erasable line. You may also want to draw a large circle on the chalkboard.

   b. Using the data above, dogs would fill $\frac{1}{2}$ of the graph, and cats would fill $\frac{1}{4}$ of the graph. Draw dark lines to define those sections.

   c. Lightly divide the remaining fourth into five equal sections. The turtles, birds, and mice each fill one section, and snakes fill up two sections. Record the information.

   d. Color each section a different color and give the graph a title.

3. Go over the *Sensational Surveys* reproducible with the class.

## ★ Taking It Farther

Have students monitor their activities for 24 hours and record the data on a circle graph. Divide a circle into 24 equal parts as follows:

✳ Draw a 12-inch circle on poster paper and cut it out.

✳ Divide the circle into sixths by folding. First, fold the circle in half. Then fold $\frac{1}{3}$ of the top half on top of the other $\frac{2}{3}$. Next fold over the other $\frac{1}{3}$. The circle is now divided into sixths.

✳ Fold this triangle twice, and the circle is divided into 24 equal parts.

## ✔ Assessing Skills

✳ Do students understand that adding all the fractional parts of a circle graph equals 1?

✳ Do students use equivalent fractions to help them divide the circle graph more accurately?

### LEARNING OBJECTIVE

Students compare and order fractions.

### GROUPING

Cooperative groups of 3 or 4

### MATERIALS

For each group:

✳ markers

✳ crayons or colored pencils

✳ poster paper

✳ 12-inch cardboard circle

✳ scissors

✳ colored chalk

✳ *Sensational Surveys* reproducible (p. 16)

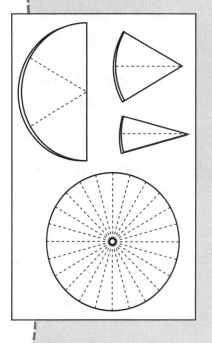

# Sensational Surveys

This is your chance to get the scoop on your classmates. Find out who likes anchovies, who has a pet alligator, or who hates spiders. You design the survey, ask the questions, graph the data, and share the results.

## CHOOSING A TOPIC

1. Brainstorm survey topics. Remember to keep the ideas simple. Record your ideas on a sheet of paper.

2. Write your survey topic.

   _____

3. Write the exact questions you will be asking on a separate sheet of paper. (Each question should be specific. What is your favorite color, for instance, is a general question. Which color do you like best— red, blue, or green, is a specific question.)

## CONDUCTING THE SURVEY

Assign a job to each group member.

* **Speaker:** This person tells the class what the survey questions will be.

   _____

* **Data Collector:** This person counts the number of responses.

   _____

* **Data Recorder:** This person writes down the information.

   _____

* **Presenter:** This person is not directly involved in the survey but shares the final results with the class.

   _____

## GRAPHING THE DATA

1. Write the data collected in fractional form. For instance, if 5 people out of 20 surveyed liked the color red, the fraction would be $\frac{5}{20}$, or $\frac{1}{4}$.

2. Transfer the data to a circle graph.

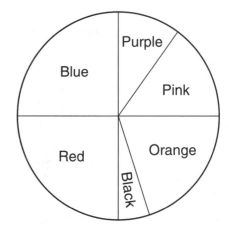

3. Give your graph a title and color it.

## SHARING THE RESULTS

The presenter shares the results of the survey with the class. The following information must be included.

* How many people were surveyed?

* Share the circle graph. Talk about each portion of the graph and tell what information is given.

* Tell what the surveyed students liked most and what they liked least.

* Tell what strategy the group used to divide the graph into representative parts.

$3\frac{1}{2} + 8\frac{1}{6} + \frac{1}{8} = ?$ ✳ $\frac{1}{2} = \frac{2}{4} = \frac{4}{8}$ ✳ $0.5 = 0.50 = 0.500$ ✳ $123.45$

**Fractions: Comparing & Ordering**

# Fraction Line-Up

**Students race to get their fractions in order from least to greatest before their opponents beat them to it!**

## ⟳→ Directions

1. Tell students they will be playing a game. The goal is to order fractions from least to greatest before their opponent does.

2. Distribute half an egg carton to each student and a set of cards to each pair.

3. Direct pairs to sit facing each other with the draw pile of fraction cards facedown between them. They place the "least fraction" card next to the far left section of the egg carton and the "greatest fraction" card next to the far right section.

4. Each player draws six cards, placing them from left to right in his or her egg carton as the cards are chosen. Another card is placed faceup next to the card pile. This is the discard pile.

5. In turn, a player chooses one card from either the draw or discard pile. That card may be used to improve the least-to-greatest order in the egg carton. If the card drawn is used, the replaced card is discarded. If the card drawn is not used, it is discarded. Cards already in the egg carton can never be moved from one cup to another. The turn ends when player discards the unused or replaced card.

6. If a player draws a card that is equivalent to a fraction in his or her egg carton, this is considered a bonus card. The player may discard the card and take two free turns in a row.

7. The first player who can put the fractions in order wins the game.

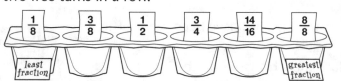

8. Save these egg cartons for the *Name That Decimal* activity on page 37 and the *Guess That Decimal* activity on page 38.

## ☆ Taking It Farther

Increase the level of difficulty by adding cards with improper fractions and fractions with many different denominators.

## ✓ Assessing Skills

Are students developing strategies? Are they spacing fractions so there is a high probability that they can fill the sections that are out of order?

**LEARNING OBJECTIVE**

Students compare and order fractions with like and unlike denominators.

**GROUPING**

Pairs

**MATERIALS**

✳ marker
✳ scissors

For each pair:

✳ 1 egg carton
✳ 40 index cards
✳ paper and pencils

**ADVANCE PREPARATION**

1. Remove the lid of the egg carton, and cut the base in half lengthwise so that you have two separate rows with six sections.

2. Cut the index cards into 1-inch by 2-inch strips and write the following fractions on one side:

$\frac{1}{2}, \frac{2}{2}, \frac{1}{4}, \frac{2}{4}, \frac{3}{4}, \frac{4}{4},$

$\frac{1}{8}, \frac{2}{8}, \frac{3}{8}, \frac{4}{8}, \frac{5}{8}, \frac{6}{8}, \frac{7}{8}, \frac{8}{8},$

from $\frac{1}{16}$ to $\frac{16}{16}$ ($\frac{1}{16}, \frac{2}{16}, \ldots$),

from $\frac{1}{32}$ to $\frac{10}{32}$ ($\frac{1}{32}, \frac{2}{32}, \ldots$).

You also may let students create the cards.

3. For each egg carton, write two cards, "least fraction" and "greatest fraction."

# Shoot for the Stars

**This fraction game doubles as a bulletin board and can be displayed all year.**

## ⟲→ Directions

1. Give two white stars to each student. Have students write an improper fraction on one star. On the other star they write the corresponding mixed number. They should not rename the mixed number in lowest terms.

2. Mix the white stars and tack each one facedown to a yellow star on the bulletin board. Place the white stars randomly.

3. Divide the class into two even teams and decide which team will go first. If you have an odd number of students in your class, choose one student to be the scorekeeper. If not, take that role yourself.

4. The players must match improper fractions to their equivalent mixed numbers. They choose two white stars and read the fractions aloud. If there is a match, remove the white stars from the bulletin board. The scorekeeper gives one point to the team. Then the other team takes a turn.

5. The game continues until all of the matches have been made. The team with more points wins.

6. At the end of the game, replace the white stars on the bulletin board.

## ☆ Taking It Farther

This game can be adapted to any subject or theme. Students may enjoy matching vocabulary words to definitions, decimal names to their numeric equivalent, or geometric shapes to their names.

## ✓ Assessing Skills

Are students reversing the numerator and denominator? If so, the initial use of concrete models can help eliminate this error.

---

### LEARNING OBJECTIVE

Students change improper fractions to mixed numbers and mixed numbers to improper fractions.

### GROUPING

Whole class

### MATERIALS

* yellow construction paper
* white paper
* black markers
* scissors
* stapler
* thumb tacks
* cardboard or star cookie cutter for star template

### ADVANCE PREPARATION

1. Make a star template out of cardboard or use a cookie cutter to trace 28 stars on yellow construction paper. Cut out the stars. Laminate them if you want.

2. Staple the 28 yellow stars to the bulletin board as placeholders.

3. Trace 28 stars on white paper and cut them out.

$3\frac{1}{2} + 8\frac{1}{6} + \frac{1}{8} = ?$ ✳ $\frac{1}{2} = \frac{2}{4} = \frac{4}{8}$ ✳ $0.5 = 0.50 = 0.500$ ✳ $123.45$

**Mixed Numbers**

# The Great Fraction Race

**This outdoor game will inspire even the most reluctant math students.**

## ⟶ Directions

1. Divide the class into groups of 5 or 6.

2. Write the following whole and mixed numbers on the board vertically:

   $3\frac{2}{7}$, $3$, $9\frac{1}{2}$, $7$, $2\frac{1}{9}$, $4\frac{2}{9}$, $9$, $4$, $6\frac{1}{4}$, $10\frac{2}{8}$, $8$, $3$, $9\frac{5}{7}$, $4\frac{9}{12}$, $5$, $1\frac{6}{7}$, $4\frac{1}{7}$, $7\frac{1}{11}$, $7\frac{2}{9}$, $19\frac{2}{4}$, $9\frac{1}{4}$, $13\frac{1}{5}$, $4$, $2$, $3\frac{2}{9}$, $20$, $9\frac{6}{9}$, $2\frac{4}{5}$, $2$, and $4\frac{5}{7}$

   One member of each group copies them on a piece of notebook paper.

3. Take students to the playground and give them the start signal. The objective is for each group to find as many hidden milk cartons as possible. Then they write the improper fraction found in the milk carton beside the corresponding number on their number list. (The mixed number has not been renamed in lowest terms.)

4. After the group completes the task, each member sits down.

5. When all of the groups are sitting down, the group with the largest number of correct matches wins the game. That group hides the milk cartons for the next, or a future, game.

## ⭐ Taking It Farther

Here are two variations on the game:

✳ Play the game with two sets of fractions that equal the number 1.

✳ Have students match a set of fractions that, when reduced, equals the other set.

## ✓ Assessing Skills

✳ Are students working cooperatively to complete the task?

✳ Can students change a mixed number to an improper fraction without first looking at the improper fractions on the list?

### LEARNING OBJECTIVE

Students match improper fractions to equivalent mixed numbers.

### GROUPING

Cooperative groups of 5 or 6

### MATERIALS

✳ 30 empty milk cartons
✳ several sheets of notebook paper
✳ scissors
✳ markers

### ADVANCE PREPARATION

1. Cut a piece of notebook paper into 30 narrow strips along the writing lines.

2. Write one of the following fractions on each strip of paper:

   $\frac{23}{7}$, $\frac{15}{5}$, $\frac{19}{2}$, $\frac{28}{4}$, $\frac{19}{9}$, $\frac{38}{9}$, $\frac{27}{3}$,
   $\frac{16}{4}$, $\frac{25}{4}$, $\frac{82}{8}$, $\frac{88}{11}$, $\frac{75}{25}$, $\frac{68}{7}$, $\frac{57}{12}$,
   $\frac{45}{9}$, $\frac{13}{7}$, $\frac{29}{7}$, $\frac{78}{11}$, $\frac{65}{9}$, $\frac{78}{4}$, $\frac{37}{4}$,
   $\frac{66}{5}$, $\frac{100}{25}$, $\frac{12}{6}$, $\frac{29}{9}$, $\frac{80}{4}$, $\frac{87}{9}$, $\frac{14}{5}$,
   $\frac{50}{25}$, $\frac{33}{7}$

3. Place a fraction strip in each milk carton and close the top. Hide the milk cartons on the playground.

# Four in a Row Fractions

This fast-action game pairs addition and subtraction of fractions with problem-solving strategies to create a winning combination.

## ⟲→ Directions

1. Duplicate the *Four in a Row Fractions* reproducible for each pair of students.

2. Give students the following oral instructions:

   a. The game is played by two players. Decide who will go first and which kind of bean each of you will use.

   b. The first player searches for two fractions in the boxes at the top of the page that when added or subtracted equal one of the fractions on the game board. Answers are always in lowest terms.

   c. Each fraction can be used only once. Draw lines through the fractions used.

   d. After locating the fraction on the game board, the first player covers that space with a bean.

   e. The second player takes a turn. Players alternate turns.

   f. The first player to cover a row horizontally, vertically, or diagonally with his or her beans wins.

## ☆ Taking It Farther

For an extra challenge, make your own fraction boxes and game board that use unlike fractions.

## ✓ Assessing Skills

Do students randomly add or subtract fractions, hoping to find one that is on the game board? Or do they look at the board and try to find fractions that, when added or subtracted, provide the needed answers?

### LEARNING OBJECTIVE

Students add and subtract like fractions.

### GROUPING

Pairs

### MATERIALS

✳ *Four in a Row Fractions* reproducible (p. 21)

✳ 16 dried beans (8 of one kind, 8 of a different kind)

### ANSWERS

**Possible Answers:**

First row, from left:
$\frac{4}{4} - \frac{1}{4} = \frac{3}{4}$; $\frac{4}{6} - \frac{3}{6} = \frac{1}{6}$;
$\frac{7}{9} - \frac{2}{9} = \frac{5}{9}$; $\frac{9}{10} - \frac{2}{10} = \frac{7}{10}$

Second row, from left:
$\frac{1}{3} + \frac{1}{3} = \frac{2}{3}$; $\frac{3}{13} + \frac{4}{13} = \frac{7}{13}$;
$\frac{3}{12} + \frac{4}{12} = \frac{7}{12}$; $\frac{5}{18} - \frac{4}{18} = \frac{1}{18}$

Third row, from left:
$\frac{3}{7} + \frac{1}{7} = \frac{4}{7}$; $\frac{2}{5} - \frac{1}{5} = \frac{1}{5}$;
$\frac{7}{50} + \frac{12}{50} = \frac{19}{50}$; $\frac{5}{8} - \frac{1}{8} = \frac{4}{8} = \frac{1}{2}$

Fourth row, from left:
$\frac{11}{12} - \frac{1}{12} = \frac{10}{12} = \frac{5}{6}$;
$\frac{1}{30} + \frac{7}{30} = \frac{8}{30} = \frac{4}{15}$;
$\frac{3}{15} + \frac{2}{15} = \frac{5}{15} = \frac{1}{3}$;
$\frac{3}{8} - \frac{1}{8} = \frac{2}{8} = \frac{1}{8}$

# Four in a Row Fractions

Can you add and subtract fractions at lightning speed? Do you have mighty powers of logic and reasoning to help you develop game strategies? This fast action game will put your skills to the ultimate test.

**To play the game, follow your teacher's instructions.**

| $\dfrac{4}{12}$ | $\dfrac{4}{18}$ | $\dfrac{1}{8}$ | $\dfrac{7}{50}$ | $\dfrac{5}{18}$ | $\dfrac{1}{30}$ | $\dfrac{7}{9}$ | $\dfrac{1}{8}$ | $\dfrac{1}{3}$ |
|---|---|---|---|---|---|---|---|---|
| $\dfrac{5}{6}$ | $\dfrac{9}{10}$ | $\dfrac{3}{7}$ | $\dfrac{4}{13}$ | $\dfrac{3}{4}$ | $\dfrac{2}{6}$ | $\dfrac{1}{3}$ | $\dfrac{3}{6}$ | $\dfrac{2}{10}$ |
| $\dfrac{4}{4}$ | $\dfrac{5}{8}$ | $\dfrac{3}{15}$ | $\dfrac{1}{12}$ | $\dfrac{4}{6}$ | $\dfrac{3}{8}$ | $\dfrac{11}{12}$ | $\dfrac{2}{9}$ | $\dfrac{3}{12}$ |
| $\dfrac{2}{15}$ | $\dfrac{3}{13}$ | $\dfrac{1}{7}$ | $\dfrac{12}{50}$ | $\dfrac{1}{4}$ | $\dfrac{2}{5}$ | $\dfrac{7}{30}$ | $\dfrac{1}{5}$ | |

| | | | |
|---|---|---|---|
| $\dfrac{3}{4}$ | $\dfrac{1}{6}$ | $\dfrac{5}{9}$ | $\dfrac{7}{10}$ |
| $\dfrac{2}{3}$ | $\dfrac{7}{13}$ | $\dfrac{7}{12}$ | $\dfrac{1}{18}$ |
| $\dfrac{4}{7}$ | $\dfrac{1}{5}$ | $\dfrac{19}{50}$ | $\dfrac{1}{2}$ |
| $\dfrac{5}{6}$ | $\dfrac{4}{15}$ | $\dfrac{1}{3}$ | $\dfrac{1}{4}$ |

# Shout It Out!

This exhilarating, fast-paced fraction game will bedazzle students from start to finish.

## ➔ Directions

1. Distribute at least one fraction sentence to each student. (Give the sentences with an asterisk to advanced students.) Depending upon the number of students in the class, add or delete fraction sentences at the end.

2. The student with the beginning sentence reads it aloud. Emphasize that students must listen carefully and respond quickly, and that *only* the student with the correct answer should "Shout it out."

3. If several seconds have passed and no one has responded, say, "Who has it? Shout it out!"

4. If the holder of the sentence still fails to respond, read the previous sentence again.

5. Play until the last sentence is read.

## ★ Taking It Farther

Challenge students to make a set of Shout It Out cards for adding and subtracting fractions with unlike denominators.

## ✓ Assessing Skills

Do any students seem confused or unable to concentrate? Some visual learners may benefit from writing the sentences down as they are read.

### LEARNING OBJECTIVE

Students add and subtract like fractions.

### GROUPING

Whole class

### MATERIALS

✳ one photocopy of page 23
✳ scissors
✳ 23 index cards, tape (optional)

### ADVANCE PREPARATION

Cut apart the fraction sentences on the photocopy of page 23. You may want to let students tape the sentences to index cards for durability.

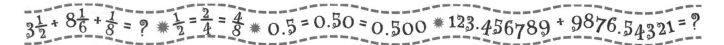

$3\frac{1}{2} + 8\frac{1}{6} + \frac{1}{8} = ?$ ✸ $\frac{1}{2} = \frac{2}{4} = \frac{4}{8}$ ✸ $0.5 = 0.50 = 0.500$ ✸ $123.456789 + 9876.54321 = ?$

# Shout It Out!

**Beginning Card**

| | | |
|---|---|---|
| My fraction is $\frac{2}{30}$.<br>Who has $\frac{2}{30}$ and $\frac{2}{30}$ more? | My fraction is $\frac{4}{30}$.<br>Who has $\frac{4}{30}$ and $\frac{5}{30}$ more? | My fraction is $\frac{9}{30}$.<br>Who has $\frac{9}{30}$ and $\frac{2}{30}$ more? |
| My fraction is $\frac{11}{30}$.<br>Who has $\frac{11}{30}$ and $\frac{5}{30}$ more? | My fraction is $\frac{16}{30}$.<br>Who has $\frac{16}{30}$ and $\frac{5}{30}$ more? | My fraction is $\frac{21}{30}$.<br>Who has $\frac{21}{30}$ and $\frac{4}{30}$ more? |
| My fraction is $\frac{25}{30}$.<br>Who has $\frac{25}{30}$ in lowest terms? | ✸ My fraction is $\frac{5}{6}$.<br>Who has $\frac{5}{6}$ and $\frac{1}{6}$ less? | My fraction is $\frac{4}{6}$.<br>Who has $\frac{4}{6}$ and $\frac{1}{6}$ less? |
| My fraction is $\frac{3}{6}$.<br>Who has $\frac{3}{6}$ and $\frac{2}{6}$ less? | My fraction is $\frac{1}{6}$.<br>Who has $\frac{1}{6}$ and $\frac{2}{6}$ more? | My fraction is $\frac{3}{6}$.<br>Who has $\frac{3}{6}$ in lowest terms? |
| ✸ My fraction is $\frac{1}{2}$.<br>Who has $\frac{1}{2}$ and $\frac{1}{2}$ more? | My fraction is $\frac{2}{2}$.<br>Who has $\frac{2}{2}$ as a<br>whole number? | My number is 1.<br>Who has 1 and $\frac{5}{16}$ less? |
| ✸ My fraction is $\frac{11}{16}$.<br>Who has $\frac{11}{16}$ and $\frac{2}{16}$ more? | My fraction is $\frac{13}{16}$.<br>Who has $\frac{13}{16}$ and $\frac{1}{16}$ more? | My fraction is $\frac{14}{16}$.<br>Who has $\frac{14}{16}$ in lowest terms? |
| ✸ My fraction is $\frac{7}{8}$.<br>Who has $\frac{7}{8}$ and $\frac{1}{8}$ less? | My fraction is $\frac{6}{8}$.<br>Who has $\frac{6}{8}$ and $\frac{1}{8}$ less? | My fraction is $\frac{5}{8}$.<br>Who has $\frac{5}{8}$ and $\frac{1}{8}$ less? |
| My fraction is $\frac{4}{8}$.<br>Who has $\frac{4}{8}$ in lowest terms? | ✸ My fraction is $\frac{1}{2}$.<br>We are done!<br>Want to start again? | **Last Card** |

# Teacher Troubles

Students solve addition and subtraction fraction problems while they unravel a riddle.

## ⚙➔ Directions

1. Duplicate the reproducible for each student.

2. Review with students addition and subtraction of fractions with unlike denominators.

| Step 1 | Step 2 | Step 3 |
|---|---|---|
| Find the common denominator. | Find the equivalent fractions. | Add or subtract. |
| $\frac{3}{8} = \frac{}{8}$ $+ \frac{1}{2} = \frac{}{8}$ | $\frac{3}{8} = \frac{3}{8}$ $+ \frac{1}{2} = \frac{4}{8}$ | $\frac{3}{8}$ $+ \frac{4}{8}$ $\overline{\frac{7}{8}}$ |

3. Students should be able to complete the reproducible on their own.

## ★ Taking It Farther

✳ Challenge students to add fractions whose sum is greater than 1.

✳ Advanced students may apply the same concepts used in this lesson to solve this fraction magic square. Each row, column, and diagonal must have the sum of 1. [All squares can be filled with $\frac{4}{12}$.]

| | | |
|---|---|---|
| $\frac{1}{3}$ | $\frac{4}{12}$ | |
| $\frac{2}{6}$ | | |
| | | $\frac{5}{15}$ |

## ✔ Assessing Skills

✳ Are students using the least common denominator (LCD)?

✳ Do students realize that in some exercises one of the fractions contains the LCD so that only the other fraction needs to be renamed?

# Teacher Troubles

Teachers never want to see these animals in their classes unless, of course, they can watch them every minute of the day. Which animals aren't trustworthy?

**Add or subtract the fractions. Rename if necessary. Next to the answer space is a letter. When you find your answer in the riddle box, place that letter above it to solve the riddle.**

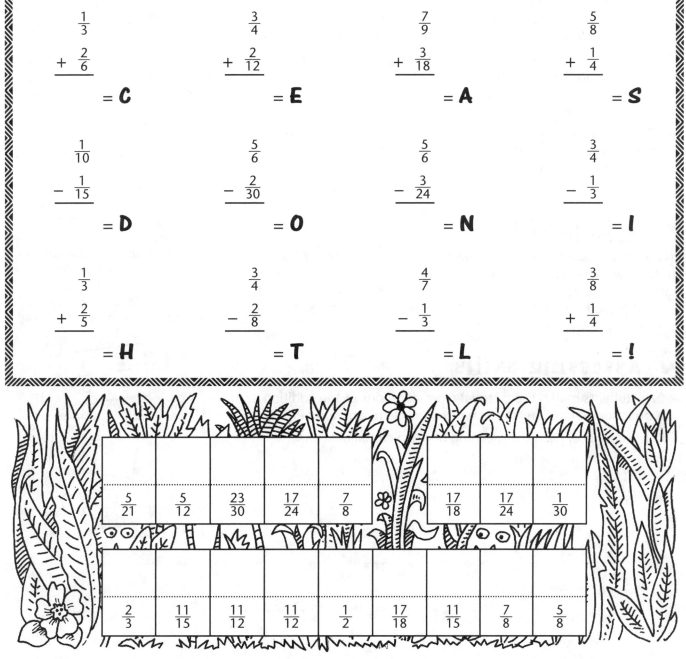

$$\frac{1}{3} + \frac{2}{6} = \textbf{C}$$

$$\frac{3}{4} + \frac{2}{12} = \textbf{E}$$

$$\frac{7}{9} + \frac{3}{18} = \textbf{A}$$

$$\frac{5}{8} + \frac{1}{4} = \textbf{S}$$

$$\frac{1}{10} - \frac{1}{15} = \textbf{D}$$

$$\frac{5}{6} - \frac{2}{30} = \textbf{O}$$

$$\frac{5}{6} - \frac{3}{24} = \textbf{N}$$

$$\frac{3}{4} - \frac{1}{3} = \textbf{I}$$

$$\frac{1}{3} + \frac{2}{5} = \textbf{H}$$

$$\frac{3}{4} - \frac{2}{8} = \textbf{T}$$

$$\frac{4}{7} - \frac{1}{3} = \textbf{L}$$

$$\frac{3}{8} + \frac{1}{4} = \textbf{!}$$

| $\frac{5}{21}$ | $\frac{5}{12}$ | $\frac{23}{30}$ | $\frac{17}{24}$ | $\frac{7}{8}$ | | $\frac{17}{18}$ | $\frac{17}{24}$ | $\frac{1}{30}$ |

| $\frac{2}{3}$ | $\frac{11}{15}$ | $\frac{11}{12}$ | $\frac{11}{12}$ | $\frac{1}{2}$ | $\frac{17}{18}$ | $\frac{11}{15}$ | $\frac{7}{8}$ | $\frac{5}{8}$ |

# Fraction Trios

**Adding and subtracting fractions is fun and easy to understand after you've played a few hands of Fraction Trios!**

## ⟳→ Directions

1. Explain that the goal of the game is to get two three-card sets before the opponent does. Each set consists of an addition or subtraction sentence, the corresponding answer, and a picture.

2. Distribute the sets of index cards to pairs. Ask them to shuffle the cards and place them in a pile. Each player chooses six cards.

3. Players take turns drawing cards from the pile. If a player chooses to keep the card he or she draws, one card must be discarded from that player's hand. The next player can then draw one card from the pile or take the discarded card.

4. The first player to get two three-card sets calls the game. The player displays the hand for the opponent to see. Before a winner is declared, both players must agree that the mathematics is correct.

## ☆ Taking It Farther

Play a similar game with mixed-number pairs. On one set of 15 cards, students write problems for multiplication of two mixed numbers. On the other set of 15 cards, they write the answers to the problems. The game is played the same way. The first person to have three two-card sets wins the game.

## ✔ Assessing Skills

✱ Can students match the pictorial representations of the addition and subtraction of fractions to the written problems and answers?

✱ Can students explain the meaning of the pictorial models?

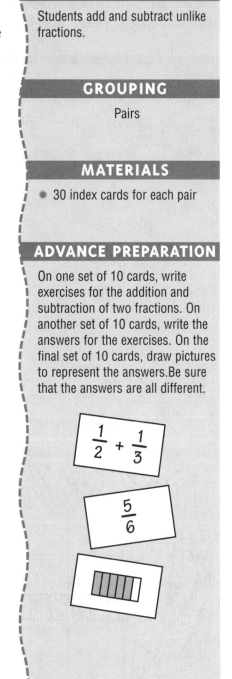

**LEARNING OBJECTIVE**

Students add and subtract unlike fractions.

**GROUPING**

Pairs

**MATERIALS**

✱ 30 index cards for each pair

**ADVANCE PREPARATION**

On one set of 10 cards, write exercises for the addition and subtraction of two fractions. On another set of 10 cards, write the answers for the exercises. On the final set of 10 cards, draw pictures to represent the answers. Be sure that the answers are all different.

$3\frac{1}{2} + 8\frac{1}{6} + \frac{1}{8} = ?$ ✳ $\frac{1}{2} = \frac{2}{4} = \frac{4}{8}$ ✳ $0.5 = 0.50 = 0.500$ ✳ $123.45$

**Fractions:
Multiplication
& Division**

# Tangram Fractions

**Add variety to your mathematics instruction with this art project that not only encourages creativity but also teaches students to multiply and divide fractions.**

## ➤ Directions

1. Review multiplication and division of fractions. Write examples such as the following on the board:

$$\frac{2}{3} \times \frac{1}{5} \qquad \frac{1}{6} \div \frac{5}{6}$$

2. Ask volunteers to show the steps in solving each example. In the multiplication example, they should point out that first the numerators are multiplied and then the denominators are multiplied. For division, students may use common denominators or multiply by the reciprocal of the divisor (e.g., $\frac{1}{6} \times \frac{6}{5}$) and reduce the fraction to lowest terms.

3. Distribute a copy of the reproducible to each student and go over the directions with the class. You may want to cut out the tangram pieces and either show how to create the swan yourself or call on volunteers to do so.

4. After students have constructed their designs, direct them to trace around the outer outlines on construction paper. Encourage them to give titles to their designs and sign their masterpieces. Trace over the lines with a black marker. Laminate the finished products and place them in your math learning center with sets of tangram pieces. Students will enjoy puzzling over their classmates' tangram creations.

## ⭐ Taking It Farther

Have students work in cooperative groups and combine tangram designs to create an amusement park, playground, or city. They can even use tangram designs to illustrate books the class is studying in literature.

## ✔ Assessing Skills

* Are students placing a problem and solution at every meeting point?
* When students divide by common fractions, do they understand that the quotient may be larger than the dividend?

### LEARNING OBJECTIVE

Students multiply and divide fractions.

### GROUPING

Individual

### MATERIALS

* black marker

For each student:
* *Tangram Fractions* reproducible (p. 28)
* one zippered plastic bag
* scissors
* construction paper

# Tangram Fractions

A tangram is an ancient Chinese puzzle with seven pieces. For centuries people have been using tangrams to create shapes and designs. Today it's your turn!

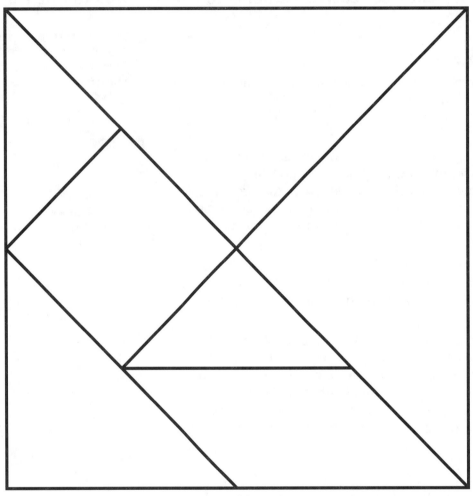

1. Use all seven tangram pieces to create a design or a shape. Each piece should share part of a side with another piece. The swan design fits the requirements. The shaded pieces on the rabbit don't meet the requirements.

2. Locate the places on your design where two pieces touch. On one side of the meeting point, write a multiplication or division problem using only fractions. On the other side of the meeting point, write the answer. Make sure you have a problem and answer at every meeting place. (See the swan diagram.)

3. Place your tangram pieces in a zippered bag. Give it to another student. He or she can pair the problems with the correct answers and reconstruct your design or picture!

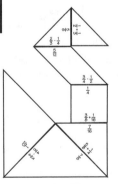

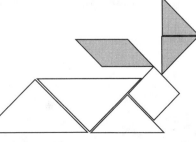

$3\frac{1}{2} + 8\frac{1}{6} + \frac{1}{8} = ?$ ✳ $\frac{1}{2} = \frac{2}{4} = \frac{4}{8}$ ✳ $0.5 = 0.50 = 0.500$ ✳ $123.45$

**Fractions: Multiplication & Division**

# Ladybug Fractions

**Students soar to new heights of understanding as they create their own ladybug fractions.**

## ➤ Directions

1. Duplicate the reproducible for each group.

2. Divide the class into groups of 4 or 5 and pass out the materials. Have a volunteer in each group cut out the pattern. Each member of the group makes a ladybug.

3. Students trace the pattern onto construction paper as indicated by color and cut out the construction paper. They glue three small circles to each wing and then punch a hole in the areas indicated on the pattern. Finally, students attach the wings and the body with the paper fastener.

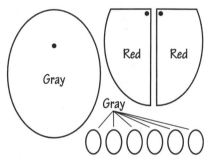

4. Ask students to write a fraction multiplication problem in the circles on one wing. Have them write a fraction division problem in the circles on the other wing.

5. Show students how to pull back each wing and write the answer to the fraction problems.

6. Attach the ladybugs to pieces of yarn and display them in the classroom. Periodically during the day have students solve the problems.

7. The activity *Don't Let Fractions Drive You Buggy* (p. 31) is an interactive bulletin board that uses the ladybugs constructed in this activity.

## ☆ Taking It Farther

Ask students to write a lowest-term fraction under the wing of the ladybug. Then challenge them to write three equivalent fractions on the circles attached to the wings.

## ✔ Assessing Skills

Do students understand that when they divide common fractions the quotient may be larger than the dividend?

### LEARNING OBJECTIVE

Students multiply and divide fractions.

### GROUPING

Cooperative groups of 4 or 5

### MATERIALS

For each group:
* *Ladybug Fractions* reproducible (p. 30)
* scissors
* glue
* markers

For each student:
* 1 sheet of red construction paper
* 1 sheet of gray construction paper
* 1 brass paper fastener
* yarn

# Ladybug Fractions

Each time the ladybug flies home, she reveals the answers to the math problems written on her wings.

**Cut out the pattern and trace it on construction paper. Punch a hole in the pattern as shown. Attach the wings to the body with a brass paper fastener. Now you're ready to write your multiplication and division problems.**

$3\frac{1}{2} + 8\frac{1}{6} + \frac{1}{8} = ?$ ✳ $\frac{1}{2} = \frac{2}{4} = \frac{4}{8}$ ✳ $0.5 = 0.50 = 0.500$ ✳ $123.45$

**Fractions:**
**Multiplication**
**& Division**

# Don't Let Fractions Drive You Buggy

This interactive bulletin board gets the whole class involved in a lively game of multiplying fractions.

## ➤ Directions

1. Ask the class to choose a game leader. Then divide the class into two even teams and assign a scorekeeper to each team. Each team tries to be the first to spell the word *ladybug.* Each scorekeeper draws seven lines on the chalkboard. As the team accumulates letters, the scorekeeper puts the letters on the lines to spell the word *ladybug.*

2. Decide which team will go first. The first player on that team chooses a ladybug and computes the answer to the problem. (Once a ladybug has been used, it can not be chosen again.)

3. The game leader pulls back the ladybug's wings and verifies that the answer is correct.

4. The letter next to the correct answer goes to that player's team. The scorekeeper writes the letter on the appropriate line. If the team already has that letter, the scorekeeper does not record it.

5. The game continues until one team completes the word *ladybug.*

## ☆ Taking It Farther

Have students extend the length of the game by spelling several words or a phrase. The difficult part is making words or phrases that have the same letters found in *ladybug.* Let the class experiment and have fun creating their own unique titles. One class came up with the title *Bad, Bad, Daddybug.*

## ✓ Assessing Skills

Are students renaming the fractions in lowest terms?

### LEARNING OBJECTIVE

Students multiply fractions.

### GROUPING

Whole class

### MATERIALS

✳ Ladybug constructions from the *Ladybug Fractions* activity (p. 30)

✳ poster paper

✳ white construction paper

✳ black marker

✳ thumb tacks

### ADVANCE PREPARATION

1. Cover the bulletin board with poster paper and an attractive border. Affix construction paper letters to the board that read, "Don't Let Fractions Drive You Buggy!"

2. Open the wings on the ladybug constructions. Beside each answer, write one of the following letters: L, A, D, Y, B, U, G. Distribute the letters as evenly as possible, so that there are not too many of one letter.

3. Close the wings and attach the ladybug constructions to the bulletin board.

$3\frac{1}{2} + 8\frac{1}{6} + \frac{1}{8} = ?$ ✸ $\frac{1}{2} = \frac{2}{4} = \frac{4}{8}$ ✸ $0.5 = 0.50 = 0.500$ ✸ $123.45$

**Relating Fractions with Mixed Numbers and Decimals**

# Clowning Around

**Relating fractions and decimals is sure to be a laughing matter when students shade decimal shapes and watch the clown Wearie Willie come to life!**

## ➤ Directions

1. Duplicate the reproducible for each student.

2. Review the concept of fractions and equivalent decimals. Write the following fractions and equivalent decimals in random order on the board:

   $3\frac{3}{10}$    3.3    $\frac{96}{100}$    0.96    $17\frac{8}{100}$    17.08    $\frac{9}{10}$    0.9

   Call on volunteers to match the fractions with the equivalent decimals and explain how they matched the two.

3. Allow the students to complete the page on their own.

## ✪ Taking It Farther

Students can easily make their own picture puzzles for classmates to solve. Give one piece of centimeter graph paper to each student. They may use the graph paper to sketch their pictures and then write the decimals that will fit their drawings on notebook paper. After students list the matching fractions, they exchange puzzles.

## ✔ Assessing Skills

✳ Can students differentiate between decimals such as 0.5 and 0.05?

✳ Do students realize that 1.20 and 1.2 are equivalent?

---

### LEARNING OBJECTIVE

Students match fractions with equivalent decimals.

### GROUPING

Individual

### MATERIALS

✳ *Clowning Around* reproducible (p. 33)

✳ colored pencils

✳ centimeter graph paper

### ANSWERS

The shapes with the following decimals should be shaded: 0.3, 0.25, 16.5, 1.2, 0.14, 4.49, 0.7, 0.07, 15.8, 0.71, 3.3, 33.9.

# Clowning Around

What do Wearie Willie and the man Emmett Kelly have in common? They're different names for the same person. Emmett Kelly spent hours putting on makeup to magically transform himself into the sad circus clown known as Wearie Willie.

**Create your own transformation. Match the fractions in the data bank with the equivalent decimals in the picture puzzle and then shade them. The first one has been done for you.**

**DATA BANK**

$\frac{3}{10}$  $\frac{25}{100}$

$16\frac{5}{10}$  $1\frac{2}{10}$

$\frac{14}{100}$  $4\frac{49}{100}$

$\frac{7}{10}$  $\frac{7}{100}$

$15\frac{8}{10}$  $3\frac{3}{10}$

$\frac{71}{100}$  $33\frac{9}{10}$

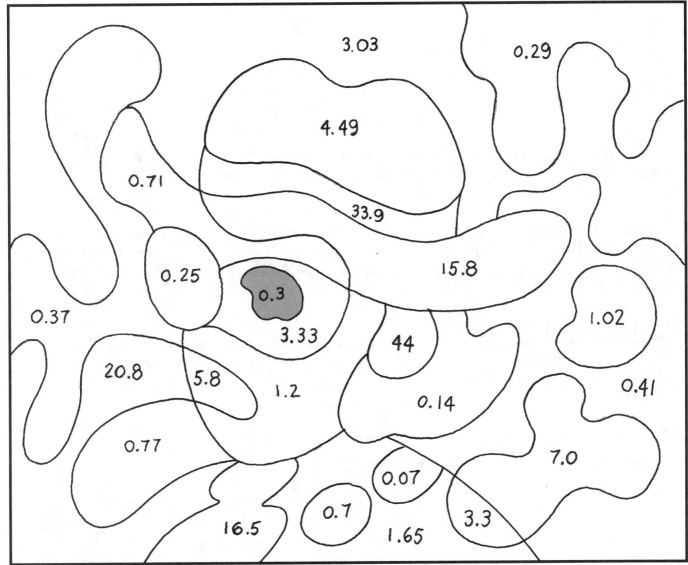

$3\frac{1}{2} + 8\frac{1}{6} + \frac{1}{8} = ?$ ✶ $\frac{1}{2} = \frac{2}{4} = \frac{4}{8}$ ✶ $0.5 = 0.50 = 0.500$ ✶ $123.45$

**Relating Fractions with Mixed Numbers and Decimals**

# Battling Decimals

Two players match wits and try to be the first to cross a fraction game board.

## ⟶ Directions

1. Explain to students that the goal of the game is to make a path with their game cards across the game board before their opponent does. Decimal game cards must be placed on corresponding fraction and mixed number squares. Each piece must be connected by at least a corner. You may want to show the following arrangements using game boards and game cards.

**Vertical Path**

| $1\frac{1}{10}$ | 0.4 | $12\frac{7}{100}$ | $\frac{5}{10}$ | $193\frac{1}{10}$ |
|---|---|---|---|---|
| $6\frac{5}{100}$ | $\frac{1}{10}$ | 56.1 | $\frac{3}{10}$ | $\frac{1}{100}$ |
| $\frac{9}{100}$ | 6.4 | $16\frac{8}{1000}$ | $\frac{6}{10}$ | $\frac{16}{100}$ |
| $8\frac{2}{100}$ | 1.9 | $5\frac{4}{1000}$ | $9\frac{3}{10}$ | $\frac{47}{100}$ |
| $57\frac{2}{10}$ | $\frac{7}{10}$ | 3.16 | $6\frac{2}{10}$ | $1\frac{57}{100}$ |

**Horizontal Path**

| $1\frac{1}{10}$ | $\frac{4}{10}$ | $12\frac{7}{100}$ | $\frac{5}{10}$ | $193\frac{1}{10}$ |
|---|---|---|---|---|
| 6.05 | $\frac{1}{10}$ | $56\frac{1}{10}$ | $\frac{3}{10}$ | $\frac{1}{100}$ |
| $\frac{9}{100}$ | 6.4 | $16\frac{8}{1000}$ | $\frac{6}{10}$ | $\frac{16}{100}$ |
| $8\frac{2}{100}$ | 1.9 | 5.004 | $9\frac{3}{10}$ | $\frac{47}{100}$ |
| $57\frac{2}{10}$ | $\frac{7}{10}$ | $3\frac{16}{100}$ | 6.2 | 1.57 |

**Incorrect Path**

| $1\frac{1}{10}$ | 0.4 | 12.07 | $\frac{5}{10}$ | $193\frac{1}{10}$ |
|---|---|---|---|---|
| $6\frac{5}{100}$ | $\frac{1}{10}$ | $56\frac{1}{10}$ | $\frac{3}{10}$ | 0.01 |
| $\frac{9}{100}$ | 6.4 | $16\frac{8}{1000}$ | $\frac{6}{10}$ | $\frac{16}{100}$ |
| $8\frac{2}{100}$ | $\frac{1}{10}$ | $5\frac{4}{1000}$ | $9\frac{3}{10}$ | 0.47 |
| $57\frac{2}{10}$ | $\frac{7}{10}$ | 3.16 | $6\frac{2}{10}$ | $1\frac{57}{100}$ |

2. Pairs shuffle the game cards and place them facedown in a pile. They also decide which player will travel horizontally and which player will travel vertically. Each player draws three cards.

3. Pairs determine who goes first. Player 1 chooses a new card from the pile and places any one of her or his four game cards on the game board. That player discards one card.

4. Player 2 takes a turn. The game continues until one player makes a path across the game board.

## ★ Taking It Farther

Follow the same directions and have students pair improper fractions to mixed numbers.

## ✓ Assessing Skills

Can students differentiate among 1.02, 1.2, and 1.20?

### LEARNING OBJECTIVE

Given fractions and mixed numbers, students match equivalent decimals.

### GROUPING

Pairs

### MATERIALS

✶ 2 pieces of tagboard
✶ thin-tipped marker
✶ scissors

### ADVANCE PREPARATION

1. To make a game board, cut tagboard to measure $8\frac{1}{2}$ by $8\frac{1}{2}$ inches. Divide the game board into 25 squares that measure $1\frac{1}{2}$ inches by $1\frac{1}{2}$ inches. Outline the squares with a thin-tipped marker.

2. To make game cards, follow the same directions and cut the squares into separate pieces.

3. Copy the numbers from the examples below onto the game board and game cards.

| $1\frac{1}{10}$ | $\frac{4}{10}$ | $12\frac{7}{100}$ | $\frac{5}{10}$ | $193\frac{1}{10}$ |
|---|---|---|---|---|
| $6\frac{5}{100}$ | $\frac{1}{10}$ | $56\frac{1}{10}$ | $\frac{3}{10}$ | $\frac{1}{100}$ |
| $\frac{9}{100}$ | $6\frac{4}{10}$ | $16\frac{8}{1000}$ | $\frac{6}{10}$ | $\frac{16}{100}$ |
| $8\frac{2}{100}$ | $1\frac{9}{10}$ | $5\frac{4}{1000}$ | $9\frac{3}{10}$ | $\frac{47}{100}$ |
| $57\frac{2}{10}$ | $\frac{7}{10}$ | $3\frac{16}{100}$ | $6\frac{2}{10}$ | $1\frac{57}{100}$ |

| 1.1 | 0.4 | 12.07 | 0.5 | 193.1 |
|---|---|---|---|---|
| 6.05 | 0.1 | 56.1 | 0.3 | 0.01 |
| 0.09 | 6.4 | 16.008 | 0.6 | 0.16 |
| 8.02 | 1.9 | 5.004 | 9.3 | 0.47 |
| 57.2 | 0.7 | 3.16 | 6.2 | 1.57 |

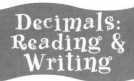

# Stumpers

Challenge students with these weekly decimal problems.

## ⟳→ Directions

1. Review decimal place value.

| Tens | Ones | Decimal Point | Tenths | Hundredths |
|------|------|---------------|--------|------------|
| 2 | 1 | . | 4 | 5 |
| 3 | 7 | . | 0 | 8 |
| | 5 | . | 6 | |

Go over how each decimal is read and written:
We say, "Twenty-one and forty-five hundredths."
We write 21.45.
We say, "Thirty-seven and eight hundredths."
We write 37.08.
We say, "Five and six tenths."
We write 5.6.

2. Students use the clues in each problem to find the mystery number.

3. They write the answers using both numbers and words. For instance, 13.97 is also written as thirteen and ninety-seven hundredths.

## ☆ Taking It Farther

Students may enjoy making their own decimal problems to stump classmates. Place the new Stumpers in your learning center.

## ✓ Assessing Skills

Are students writing six tenths as 0.06 or as 0.6? Many students incorrectly reason that since tens are two places to the left of the decimal, tenths must be two places to the right of the decimal.

# Stampers

Write your answers on a separate piece of paper in both number and word form; for example, 14.37 (number form), fourteen and thirty-seven hundredths (word form).

**A. Who Am I?**
1. I have 4 digits, and they all are different.
2. All of my digits are odd.
3. I have a 1 in the hundredths place.
4. I have a 7 in the ones place.
5. The number in the tens place is less than the number in the tenths place.
6. None of my digits are 9.

**B. Who Am I?**
1. I have 4 digits.
2. Each digit is either a 2 or a 4.
3. The numbers in the ones place and tenths place are the same.
4. The numbers in the tens place and hundredths place are the same.
5. I have a 4 in the hundredths place.

**C. Who Am I?**
1. I have 4 digits, and they are all odd.
2. The number in the tenths place is greater than 3. It is a factor of 36.
3. The number in the hundredths place is less than 4 and greater than 1.
4. The numbers in the ones and tens places are the same and are also factors of 25.

**D. Who Am I?**
1. I have 4 digits, and they are all odd.
2. The 2-digit whole number is greater than 10 and less than 20. When this number is divided into 121, the quotient is also that number.
3. The digit in the tenths place is 3.
4. Add 4 to the number in the tenths place and you will have the number in the hundredths place.

**E. Who Am I?**
1. I have 4 digits, and they are all different and even.
2. The number in the hundredths place is half of the number in the tenths place.
3. The number in the hundredths place is greater than 3.
4. The number in the ones place is 6.
5. The number in the tens place is 2.

**F. Who Am I?**
1. I am a whole number.
2. I am greater than 50.
3. I am equal to the number of days in 9 weeks, minus 48 hours.

**G. Who Am I?**
1. I have 3 even digits.
2. The number in the tenths place when subtracted from 3 equals 1.
3. The number in the ones place is 8.
4. Divide the number in the ones place by 2 and you will have the number in the hundredths place.

**H. Who Am I?**
1. I have 4 digits.
2. The numbers in the tenths and hundredths places are the same.
3. The numbers in the ones place and tens place are the same.
4. The number in the tenths place when added to 4 and subtracted from 10 is 0.
5. The number in the ones place is 4.

$3\frac{1}{2} + 8\frac{1}{6} + \frac{1}{8} = ?$ ✳ $\frac{1}{2} = \frac{2}{4} = \frac{4}{8}$ ✳ $0.5 = 0.50 = 0.500$ ✳ $123.45$

**Decimals: Reading & Writing**

# Name That Decimal

Learning decimal place value is fun and egg-citing with this simple egg carton game.

## ➤ Directions

1. Distribute egg cartons, number cubes, and dried beans to students. Have them form pairs. Explain that they will be playing a game. The goal of the game is for each player to create a greater number in her or his egg carton than her or his opponent.

2. Players roll number cubes to determine order of play; the player with the higher number goes first.

3. Player 1 rolls the number cube. Suppose a 4 is rolled. Then 4 dried beans may be put in any empty section in that player's egg carton.

4. Player 2 rolls the number cube. Suppose a 6 is rolled. Then 6 beans may be put in any empty section in that player's egg carton.

5. Play continues until all the sections in both egg cartons are filled.

6. Students write and read the number represented by the beans in their egg cartons. The player with the greater number wins the game.

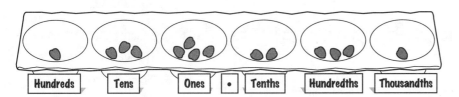

| Hundreds | Tens | Ones | • | Tenths | Hundredths | Thousandths |

**The number in the egg carton above is 134.231.**

## ★ Taking It Farther

Glue two egg cartons together, end to end, and increase the decimal to the millionths.

## ✔ Assessing Skills

✳ Are students developing a strategy or randomly placing the dried beans in the egg cartons?

✳ Do students read and write the decimals correctly?

**LEARNING OBJECTIVE**

Students read and write decimals to the thousandths.

**GROUPING**

Pairs

**MATERIALS**

✳ marker

✳ index cards

For each student:

✳ half an egg carton (Use the egg cartons from the *Fraction Line-Up* activity on page 17, or see directions for making them. Be sure to save these egg cartons and place-value labels for the *Guess That Decimal* activity on page 38.)

✳ 1 number cube labeled 1–6

✳ 30 dried beans

**ADVANCE PREPARATION**

1. Use index cards to label the sections of each egg carton from left to right as follows: Hundreds, Tens, Ones, Tenths, Hundredths, and Thousandths.

2. Place a decimal point between the Ones and Tenths.

$$3\frac{1}{2} + 8\frac{1}{6} + \frac{1}{8} = ? \quad * \quad \frac{1}{2} = \frac{2}{4} = \frac{4}{8} \quad * \quad 0.5 = 0.50 = 0.500 \quad * \quad 123.45$$

## Decimals: Place Value

# Guess That Decimal

**This guessing game helps students develop their logical-reasoning skills and teaches decimal place value.**

## Directions

1. Explain to students that they will be playing a game with partners. The goal of the game is to ask yes and no questions to determine their opponent's secret number.

2. Distribute half an egg carton and one stack of numbered cards to each student and then pair them.

3. Partners sit facing each other. They place a number card in each section of the egg carton to make a 6-digit secret number. The number on each card stands for the number of units in that place.

4. After deciding who goes first, players ask one yes or no question per turn, such as, "Is there an odd number in the ones place?" or "Is the number in the tenths place greater than 5?" Students may record responses on a separate sheet of paper.

5. The first person to correctly guess the opponent's secret number wins the game.

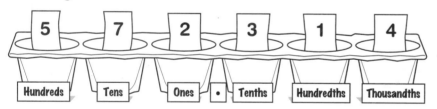

**The number in the egg carton above is 572.314.**

## Taking It Farther

Have students use the egg cartons to create more secret numbers and then develop a list of clues that will lead others to identify the number. Post the list of clues in your math learning center or on the bulletin board and see how many students can guess the correct answer.

## Assessing Skills

Are students able to formulate good questions that eliminate many possible answers?

$3\frac{1}{2} + 8\frac{1}{6} + \frac{1}{8} = ?$ ✻ $\frac{1}{2} = \frac{2}{4} = \frac{4}{8}$ ✻ $0.5 = 0.50 = 0.500$ ✻ $123.45$

## Decimals: Place Value

# Every Number Has Its Place

**Kids love a challenge. This decimal place-value puzzle will put them to the ultimate test.**

## ⟶ Directions

1. Review place value to the thousandth place with the class.

2. To familiarize students with the puzzle, present the following sample:

   a. *Use the following decimals to complete the puzzle: 7.7, 40.8, 1.3, 38.18, 137.01, 1.6, 36.7.*

   b. *Decimal points occupy one space and are already written in.*

   c. *Sort and classify the decimals before you begin to solve the puzzle.* (Students may classify the decimals in different ways. One possibility is shown below.)

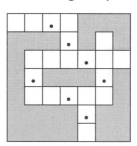

| 2 digits | 3 digits | 4 digits | 5 digits |
|----------|----------|----------|----------|
| 7.7      | 40.8     | 38.18    | 137.01   |
| 1.3      | 36.7     |          |          |
| 1.6      |          |          |          |

3. As the solution shows, by classifying and using the process of elimination, it's easy to solve the puzzle.

## ☆ Taking It Farther

Give students graph paper and have them make their own decimal puzzles.

## ✓ Assessing Skills

Are students sorting and classifying the decimals before they begin solving the puzzle?

### LEARNING OBJECTIVE

Students read and write decimals to thousandths.

### GROUPING

Individual

### MATERIALS

For each student:

✻ *Every Number Has Its Place* reproducible (p. 40)

✻ graph paper

### ANSWERS

| | |
|---|---|
| **1.** 3.44 | **9.** 1.006 |
| **2.** 4.6 | **10.** 45.63 |
| **3.** 41.7 | **11.** 15.3 |
| **4.** 4016.32 | **12.** 317.9 |
| **5.** 947.36 | **13.** 3007.55 |
| **6.** 6.5 | **14.** 6.19 |
| **7.** 56.4 | **15.** 6.99 |
| **8.** 1.35 | |

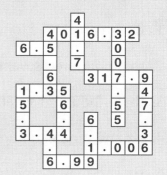

# Every Number Has Its Place

Approach this activity with caution—it's been known to produce high levels of fun and learning! Each digit can occupy only one place to make the whole puzzle fit together perfectly.

**Write each decimal in standard form on the lines below. Fit the number into the puzzle. The decimal points occupy one space and are already written in the puzzle.**

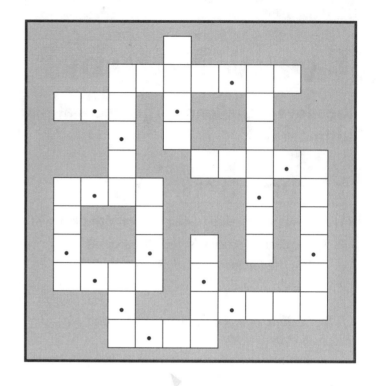

1. three and forty-four hundredths _____

2. four and six tenths _____

3. forty-one and seven tenths _____

4. four thousand sixteen and thirty-two hundredths _____

5. nine hundred forty-seven and thirty-six hundredths _____

6. six and five tenths _____

7. fifty-six and four tenths _____

8. one and thirty-five hundredths _____

9. one and six thousandths _____

10. forty-five and sixty-three hundredths _____

11. fifteen and three tenths _____

12. three hundred seventeen and nine tenths _____

13. three thousand seven and fifty-five hundredths _____

14. six and nineteen hundredths _____

15. six and ninety-nine hundredths _____

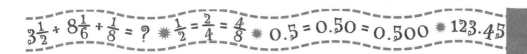

# "Weighty" Problems

Students compare and order decimals and find that none of us weighs too much—we're just living on the wrong planet!

## Directions

1. Duplicate the reproducible for each student.

2. Review comparing and ordering decimals as follows:

   a. Compare 3.67 and 3.69.

   b. Begin with the digits on the left.
   The ones and tenths are the same.

   c. Compare the hundredths: 9 hundredths > 7 hundredths.
   So 3.69 > 3.67.

3. Let students complete the reproducible on their own.

## Taking It Farther

Obtain several books on the planets. Have students research the planets and compare the diameters, distance from the sun, and temperatures.

## Assessing Skills

Are students looking at all the numbers to the left first? Some students may reason that 4,321.9 is larger than 4,322.7 because the digit in the tenths place is greater in the first number. They may fail to see that the 2 is greater than the 1 in the ones place.

**LEARNING OBJECTIVE**

Students compare and order decimals.

**GROUPING**

Individual

**MATERIALS**

* "Weighty" Problems reproducible (p. 42)

**ANSWERS**

1. a. 0.04 (Pluto)
   b. 0.38 (Mercury)
   c. 0.38 (Mars)
   d. 0.91 (Venus)
   e. 0.93 (Saturn)
   f. 0.93 (Uranus)
   g. 1.00 (Earth)
   h. 1.14 (Neptune)
   i. 2.34 (Jupiter)

2. Jupiter

3. Pluto

4. Pluto

5. Saturn and Uranus; Mercury and Mars

6. 280,000 pounds

# "Weighty" Problems

When you weigh yourself, you're really measuring how much gravity pulls on you. If you weigh 100 pounds on Earth, you'd only weigh 38 pounds on Mars. That's because the pull of gravity is less on Mars.

**The table lists the pull of gravity on the other planets as compared to Earth's. Use it to answer the "weighty" problems that follow.**

| Planet | Gravitational Pull |
|--------|--------------------|
| Mercury | 0.38 times Earth's |
| Venus | 0.91 times Earth's |
| Earth | 1.00 times Earth's |
| Mars | 0.38 times Earth's |
| Jupiter | 2.34 times Earth's |
| Saturn | 0.93 times Earth's |
| Uranus | 0.93 times Earth's |
| Neptune | 1.14 times Earth's |
| Pluto | 0.04 times Earth's |

1. Order the decimals from least to greatest. Write the name of the planet next to the decimal.

   a. _____   _____

   b. _____   _____

   c. _____   _____

   d. _____   _____

   e. _____   _____

   f. _____   _____

   g. _____   _____

   h. _____   _____

   i. _____   _____

2. On which planet would you weigh the most? _____

3. On which planet would you weigh the least? _____

4. The pull of gravity on the moon is 0.17 times Earth's. On which planet would you weigh less than you would on the moon? _____

5. On which planets would you weigh the same? _____

6. The pull of gravity on the sun is 2,800 times Earth's. A person who weighs 100 pounds on Earth would weigh _____ pounds on the sun.

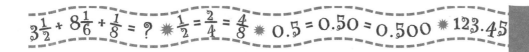
# Wacky Presidential Firsts

Ordering decimals can be an adventure when the first decimal in the group reveals the name of the president who had a pet raccoon he walked on a leash!

## Directions

1. Duplicate the *Wacky Presidential Firsts* reproducible for each student.

2. Review comparing decimals by asking students to look at place value.

   **a.** To compare 0.45 and 0.47, begin by lining up the decimal points.

   $$0.45$$
   $$0.47$$

   **b.** Compare tenths. If they are equal, compare hundredths.

   $$0.45$$
   $$0.47$$

   **c.** Compare hundredths.

   $$0.45$$
   $$0.47$$

   Since 7 > 5, 0.47 > 0.45.

## Taking It Farther

Let students poll classmates and find out who was the first student to eat sushi or do any other zany action. Encourage them to create their own math problems based on these actions.

## Assessing Skills

How do students approach problems with an uneven number of digits? Do they understand that 0.7 = 0.70?

---

### LEARNING OBJECTIVE

Students compare and order decimals to the hundredths place.

### GROUPING

Individual

### MATERIALS

* *Wacky Presidential Firsts* reproducible (p. 44)

### ANSWERS

**1.** 129.00 (Calvin Coolidge)

**2.** 42.05 (James Garfield)

**3.** 1.7 (Ulysses S. Grant)

**4.** 144.00 (Zachary Taylor)

**5.** 2.80 (Zachary Taylor)

**6.** 3.00 (Martin Van Buren)

# Wacky Presidential Firsts

These presidents go down in history not only as statesmen or for resolving international conflicts. They're also known for their offbeat actions.

**Read each fact. Order the decimals under it from greatest to least. The greatest decimal reveals the name of the notorious president who did it!**

1. Most people have pets like dogs, cats, horses, snakes, or mice—not this president! He was the first to have a raccoon for a pet. He named her Rebecca and even walked her on a leash.

   128.8 (Abraham Lincoln)

   129.00 (Calvin Coolidge)

   128.87 (Herbert Hoover)

   _____

2. This president could write in Greek with one hand and in Latin with the other—at the same time!

   42.05 (James Garfield)

   42.01 (Rutherford Hayes)

   41.07 (Jimmy Carter)

   _____

3. Can you imagine getting a speeding ticket for riding a horse too fast? He was the first president to achieve such a feat!

   1.39 (Andrew Jackson)

   0.95 (Abraham Lincoln)

   1.7 (Ulysses S. Grant)

   _____

4. This president not only rode into battle on a horse, he was the first to ride a horse sidesaddle.

   143.99 (George Washington)

   143.9 (Ulysses S. Grant)

   144.00 (Zachary Taylor)

   _____

5. This president liked his horse so much that he brought her to live at the White House. The horse ate the grass on the White House lawn!

   2.08 (Richard Nixon)

   2.78 (Jimmy Carter)

   2.80 (Zachary Taylor)

   _____

6. This president was a very small man. He was the first to stand on a table to deliver a speech.

   3.00 (Martin Van Buren)

   2.00 (William Harrison)

   2.99 (John Quincy Adams)

   _____

$3\frac{1}{2} + 8\frac{1}{6} + \frac{1}{8} = ?$ ✳ $\frac{1}{2} = \frac{2}{4} = \frac{4}{8}$ ✳ $0.5 = 0.50 = 0.500$ ✳ $123.45$

**Decimals: Comparing & Ordering**

# Who's First?

This activity fosters cooperation and builds skills in reading, writing, and ordering decimals.

## ➔ Directions

1. Divide the class evenly into groups of 4 or 5 students.

2. Tape a decimal number to each student's back.

3. Each person in the group asks yes or no questions of other group members to determine the decimal number that is on his or her back. Students may use paper and pencil to record the responses.

4. After each person has guessed his or her number, students arrange themselves so that they are standing in order from the least to the greatest decimal. At that time, they yell, "We're first!"

5. The other groups stop working, and the teacher determines if the group has met all the criteria. If not, the groups continue working until a winner is announced.

## ☆ Taking It Farther

*We're Buddies* is a decimal place-value game that uses the same materials as *Who's First?* Write decimal numbers on half of the sheets of notebook paper. The number may have any number of digits. Write equivalent decimals on the remaining sheets of notebook paper; for example 13.1 and 13.10, 3.50 and 3.500. Attach a sheet to each student's back. The student asks yes or no questions to determine the decimal number on his or her back. Then that student finds the student who has the equivalent decimal on his or her back. The first pair to find each other is the winner.

## ✔ Assessing Skills

✳ Do students identify each place by its appropriate name?

✳ Are students asking yes or no questions that eliminate large groups of numbers?

### LEARNING OBJECTIVE

Students read decimals to hundredths. They also compare and order decimals.

### GROUPING

Cooperative groups of 4 or 5

### MATERIALS

✳ masking tape
✳ notebook paper (1 piece per student)
✳ black marker
✳ paper and pencil

### ADVANCE PREPARATION

Write a decimal number on each piece of notebook paper. The numbers should have four digits with the decimal written to the hundredths place; for example, 23.98, 44.04, 16.22, 80.02.

$3\frac{1}{2} + 8\frac{1}{6} + \frac{1}{8} = ?$ ✳ $\frac{1}{2} = \frac{2}{4} = \frac{4}{8}$ ✳ $0.5 = 0.50 = 0.500$ ✳ $123.45$

## Rounding Decimals

# Decimal Roundup

Students combine their knowledge, speed, and perseverance for an unforgettable decimal roundup.

## ↻→ Directions

1. Remind students that to round a decimal to a specific place, they look at the number to the right of that place. If it is 5 or more, the number rounds up. If it is less than 5, the number remains the same.

2. Write the following table and examples on the board.

| Original number is | Round it to the nearest | Digit to the right is | Is it 5 or more? | Rounded number is |
|---|---|---|---|---|
| 97.6453 | whole number | 6 | yes | 98 |
| 97.6453 | tenth | 4 | no | 97.6 |
| 97.6453 | hundredth | 5 | yes | 97.65 |
| 97.6453 | thousandth | 3 | no | 97.645 |

3. Duplicate the *Decimal Roundup* reproducible for each group and distribute.

4. Tell students that you are looking for accuracy and speed. The first group with all the right answers wins.

5. Give the start signal and watch the learning begin!

## ★ Taking It Farther

Give students a number such as 4.78 and ask them to tell you all the numbers that could have been rounded to get this number and how they arrived at each number. [4.780, 4.781, 4.782, 4.783, 4.784, 4.775, 4.776, 4.777, 4.778, and 4.779]

## ✔ Assessing Skills

Are students able to talk about the numbers using their correct place-value names?

### LEARNING OBJECTIVE

Students round decimals to the nearest tenth, hundredth, or thousandth.

### GROUPING

Cooperative groups

### MATERIALS

✳ *Decimal Roundup* reproducible (p. 47)

### ANSWERS

1. 6.1947
2. 679.14
3. 97.416
4. 6.9174
5. 9.6147
6. 9.7246
7. 67.914 or 67.941

# Decimal Roundup

Hold on to your hat, this roundup is guaranteed to have your head spinning in circles.

**Use the digits 6, 7, 1, 4, and 9 to make each sentence true. Use all five digits in each number. Place the decimal point in one of the answer boxes.**

1. ⬜⬜⬜⬜⬜ rounded to the nearest hundredth is 6.19.

2. ⬜⬜⬜⬜⬜ rounded to the nearest tenth is 679.1.

3. ⬜⬜⬜⬜⬜ rounded to the nearest tenth is 97.4.

4. ⬜⬜⬜⬜⬜ rounded to the nearest thousandth is 6.917.

5. ⬜⬜⬜⬜⬜ rounded to the nearest thousandth is 9.615.

6. ⬜⬜⬜⬜⬜ rounded to the nearest hundredth is 9.72.

7. There are two possible answers to this question. Can you find them both?

⬜⬜⬜⬜⬜ and

⬜⬜⬜⬜⬜ rounded to the nearest tenth are 67.9.

$3\frac{1}{2} + 8\frac{1}{6} + \frac{1}{8} = ?$ ✸ $\frac{1}{2} = \frac{2}{4} = \frac{4}{8}$ ✸ $0.5 = 0.50 = 0.500$ ✸ $123.45$

**Rounding Decimals**

# Top Secret Numbers

**Students will become master detectives as they unravel clues to discover some top secret numbers.**

## ⟳→ Directions

1. Explain to groups that their goal is to be the first group to unravel the clues to discover the mystery number.

2. Distribute one clue card to each group member. Allow time for students to read their cards silently, then give the start signal.

3. Students share information about their clue with the group, but they *cannot* read the card aloud. The goal of this activity is to get students to communicate and work cooperatively to solve a problem.

4. The first team with the correct number wins the game.

## ☆ Taking It Farther

Follow the directions above for this problem.

*Card One*  My number has eleven digits. Four of my digits are decimals.

*Card Two*  One of my digits is 8. The rest of my digits are a different number, but they are all the same.

*Card Three* When you round me to the thousandths place, my final digit becomes a 5.

*Card Four*  All of my eleven digits are even.

[4,444,444.4448]

As an additional challenge, have each group write its own set of number clues. Groups trade sets of clues and solve.

## ✔ Assessing Skills

✳ Are students able to talk about the numbers using their correct place-value names?

✳ Do students understand rounding decimals well enough to get clues from the information?

$3\frac{1}{2} + 8\frac{1}{6} + \frac{1}{8} = ?$ ✸ $\frac{1}{2} = \frac{2}{4} = \frac{4}{8}$ ✸ $0.5 = 0.50 = 0.500$ ✸ $123.45$

## Equivalent Decimals

# Bag Math

This game requires speed, cooperation, and a sense of humor. Learning about decimals has never been this much fun!

## ⟶ Directions

1. Tell groups that the goal of this game is to be the first team to have all equivalent numbers in each bag.

2. Distribute the sets of bags to each group. Each group member takes one bag. Students need to face each other so they can work cooperatively.

3. Ask students to look at the contents of their paper bags. They can easily see that the decimals or fractions are not equivalent; however, if they could trade with other members of the group, they could have four equivalent numbers in each bag.

4. When you give the start signal, each student passes his or her paper bag clockwise. That person may either take a piece of paper out of the bag or put one in. After performing this task, the student passes the bag clockwise again. Students may talk during the activity, and they may look at the contents of the bag at any time. The team continues passing the bags around until one team wins the game.

## ☆ Taking It Farther

For a real challenge, place an improper fraction, a mixed number, a decimal, and a percent in each bag, for example, $\frac{11}{10}$, $1\frac{1}{10}$, 1.1 and 110%.

## ✔ Assessing Skills

Are students developing a cooperative strategy?

### LEARNING OBJECTIVE

Students pair equivalent decimals and mixed numbers.

### GROUPING

Cooperative groups of 4

### MATERIALS

✸ marker

For each group:

✸ 4 paper bags

✸ 1 sheet of paper cut into 16 pieces

### ADVANCE PREPARATION

Label each set of bags 1, 2, 3, and 4. Write the decimals or fractions listed below on separate pieces of paper and place them in the bag.

**Bag 1**: 1.3, 7.9, 90.07, 5.1

**Bag 2**: 1.30, 7.90, 90.070, 5.10

**Bag 3**: 1.300, 7.900, 90.0700, 5.100

**Bag 4**: $1\frac{3}{10}$, $7\frac{9}{10}$, $90\frac{7}{100}$, $5\frac{1}{10}$

$3\frac{1}{2} + 8\frac{1}{6} + \frac{1}{8} = ?$ ✹ $\frac{1}{2} = \frac{2}{4} = \frac{4}{8}$ ✹ $0.5 = 0.50 = 0.500$ ✹ $123.45$

## Equivalent Decimals

# Guarded Treasure

**Decimal knights guard the crown jewels while opponent knights scramble to uncover the treasure. This game is full of intrigue, suspense, and action.**

## ➤ Directions

1. Explain to students that the goal of this game is to break through their opponent's decimal guards and uncover the crown jewels.

2. Direct students to put all 12 cards, or knights, in different sections in the egg cartons. As they learn to play the game, they'll develop a strategy for card placement.

3. Tell students to place the long sides of the egg cartons together so neither player can see the other's cards. Then they decide who will go first.

4. Player 1 may move one of her or his knights into the opponent's court. If the section is empty, the knight may freely occupy the section. If the cup is occupied, the players must compare the value of the two knights. The knight with the greater value occupies the section and the other knight is taken from the game. If the knights are equal in value, both knights are removed. Any knight can overtake the crown jewels.

5. All the knights may move freely about the board, but the crown jewels must remain in one spot throughout the game.

6. For each turn, every player must make a move. A player may make only one move per turn.

7. The first player to uncover the opponent's crown jewels wins.

## ★ Taking It Farther

Play a similar game with fractions and decimals. To make the knights, write one of the following decimals or fractions on each card: 0.25, $\frac{25}{100}$, 0.5, 0.50, $\frac{50}{100}$, 0.75, $\frac{75}{100}$, 0.80, $\frac{80}{100}$, 0.99, and $\frac{99}{100}$. As they play the game, students compare the values of decimals and fractions.

## ✔ Assessing Skills

✳ Do students understand that 0.8 is equivalent to 0.80 and 0.800?

✳ Are students able to develop strategies to protect the crown jewels, or are they placing the knights randomly?

### LEARNING OBJECTIVE

Students order decimals written to the thousandths place, and identify equivalent decimals.

### GROUPING

Pairs

### MATERIALS

For each pair:
✳ 2 egg cartons
✳ 24 tagboard cards measuring 1 inch by 2 inches

### ADVANCE PREPARATION

1. Cut the lids off of both egg cartons.

2. Make two identical sets of 12 cards. You may also want to let students make their own cards. To make the decimal knights, write one of the following decimals on each card: 0.250, 0.25, 0.50, 0.5, 0.75, 0.750, 0.8, 0.80, 0.800, 0.99, and 0.990. Write "crown jewels" on the remaining card.

$3\frac{1}{2} + 8\frac{1}{6} + \frac{1}{8} = ?$ ✳ $\frac{1}{2} = \frac{2}{4} = \frac{4}{8}$ ✳ $0.5 = 0.50 = 0.500$ ✳ $123.45$

## Decimals: Addition & Subtraction

# Absolutely Magical

**Watch the excitement build as students order and subtract decimals and wait for the magical number 61.74 to appear.**

## → Directions

1. Duplicate and distribute the reproducible to each student.

2. To familiarize students with the formula, go over the problem on the *Absolutely Magical* reproducible.

3. Direct students to try two or three problems on their own.

4. Allow time for everyone to share their problems with others.

## ☆ Taking It Farther

✳ Have students predict if this formula would work without the decimal points. For instance, would the number 6,174 appear?

✳ Introduce palindromes. A *palindrome* is a number or word that is the same backward and forward. For instance, the number *373* and the word *dad* are palindromes. You can make a palindrome by continually adding the reverse digits. Sometimes it takes many steps.

$$\begin{array}{r} 82 \\ + \underline{\phantom{0}28} \\ 110 \\ + \underline{011} \\ 121 \end{array}$$

Add the reverse.

Add the reverse.

A palindrome results!

## ☑ Assessing Skills

Are students placing decimal points in a straight line before subtracting?

### LEARNING OBJECTIVE

Students order digits to create the largest and smallest possible numbers. They also subtract decimals.

### GROUPING

Whole class or individual

### MATERIALS

✳ *Absolutely Magical* reproducible (p. 52)

✳ paper and pencil

# Absolutely Magical

I'm sixty-one and seventy-four hundredths (61.74), and I am guaranteed to appear like magic whenever you follow an easy formula. Baffle your teachers, amaze your friends, and stump your families.

1. Pick any four different numbers between 0 and 9.    1, 5, 9, 6

2. Arrange them to make the greatest number possible.    9651

   Place a decimal between the two middle numbers.    96.51

3. Then arrange them to make the least number possible.    1569

   Place a decimal between the two middle numbers.    15.69

4. Subtract the numbers.
$$
\begin{array}{r}
96.51 \\
-\ 15.69 \\
\hline
80.82
\end{array}
$$

5. Use the four numbers in the difference.
   Repeat steps 2 through 4.
$$
\begin{array}{lr}
\text{(greatest number)} & 88.20 \\
\text{(least number)} - & 02.88 \\
\hline
\text{(difference)} & 85.32
\end{array}
$$

6. Repeat the steps.
$$
\begin{array}{lr}
\text{(greatest number)} & 85.32 \\
\text{(least number)} - & 23.58 \\
\hline
\text{(difference)} & 61.74
\end{array}
$$

**I told you so! I always appear sooner or later.
It doesn't matter what numbers you choose.
Try different numbers and amaze a friend or two!**

*Decimals and Fractions* Scholastic Professional Books

$3\frac{1}{2} + 8\frac{1}{6} + \frac{1}{8} = ?$ ✸ $\frac{1}{2} = \frac{2}{4} = \frac{4}{8}$ ✸ $0.5 = 0.50 = 0.500$ ✸ $123.45$

**Decimals: Addition & Subtraction**

# Shopping in the "Good Old Days"

**What's more fun than spending money on toys? Spending money on toys at 1902 prices! This activity combines logical reasoning, adding decimals, and shopping.**

## ⟳→ Directions

1. Duplicate the reproducible for each student.

2. Review adding decimals, as follows:

   **a.** Write the problem with the decimal points in a line.

   $$\begin{array}{r} \$\ \ 2.13 \\ 0.89 \\ +\,11.99 \\ \hline \end{array}$$

   **b.** Add hundredths. Trade if necessary

   $$\begin{array}{r} {\scriptstyle 2} \\ \$\ \ 2.13 \\ 0.89 \\ +\,11.99 \\ \hline 1 \end{array}$$

   **c.** Add tenths. Trade if necessary

   $$\begin{array}{r} {\scriptstyle 2\ \ 2} \\ \$\ \ 2.13 \\ 0.89 \\ +\,11.99 \\ \hline .01 \end{array}$$

   **d.** Add whole numbers.

   $$\begin{array}{r} {\scriptstyle 2\ \ 2} \\ \$\ \ 2.13 \\ 0.89 \\ +\,11.99 \\ \hline \$15.01 \end{array}$$

3. Students should be able to complete the activity on their own.

## ☆ Taking It Farther

Have students bring catalogs and advertisements from home. Give each student a piece of white construction paper, scissors, and glue. They cut out pictures of toys that equal about $5.00 and glue them to the construction paper. Ask that they record the mathematics on the paper. Compare prices and products from 1902 and the present.

## ✔ Assessing Skills

Are students adding randomly or developing strategies? Are they rounding numbers and making predictions? Are they determining sums and working backward?

### LEARNING OBJECTIVE

Students add decimals.

### GROUPING

Individual

### MATERIALS

For each student:

* *Shopping in the "Good Old Days"* reproducible (p. 54)
* catalogs and advertising circulars
* white construction paper
* scissors
* glue

### ANSWERS

**4 items for $6.00:**
Majestic Doll . . . . . . . $2.95
Toy Sewing Machine . . $2.25
China Tea Set . . . . . . . $0.75
Dominoes . . . . . . . . . $0.05

**6 items for $5.00:**
Majestic Doll . . . . . . . $2.95
Mechanical Warship . . $0.43
Laughing Camera . . . . $0.32
China Tea Set . . . . . . . $0.75
Dominoes . . . . . . . . . $0.05
Chess Game . . . . . . . . $0.50

# Shopping in the "Good Old Days"

It's hard to find a gift for $6.00 today. In 1902, that kind of money could buy four gifts or more. Look at the items in the Sears, Roebuck & Company catalog from 1902.

**Find four items that when added equal exactly $6.00. Circle the items.**

**Majestic Doll**
China doll with moving eyes. Dressed in a fine lace and ribbon-trimmed chemise. 23 inches tall.
**Price: $2.95 each**

**Mechanical Warship**
This ship runs in a circle with two detachable masts. It has a lifeboat and four cannons.
**Price: $0.43 each**

**Boys' Farm Wagon**
18-by-36-inch wagon. Has a seat, handle, and pair of hardwood shafts for dog or goat. Handsomely ornamented.
**Price: $5.00 each**

**Toy Sewing Machine**
This machine really sews and is beautifully decorated.
**Price: $2.25 each**

**Folding Checkerboard**
14-by-14-inch board.
**Price: $0.10 each**

**Dominoes**
Set of 28 pieces.
**Price: $0.05 each set**

**Chess Game**
Chess pieces in black and yellow.
**Price: $0.50 each set**

**Laughing Camera**
Look through this lens and stout people look thin and thin people look stout. More fun than going to the circus.
**Price: $0.32 each**

**Rubber Bat Balls**
2½-inch diameter.
**Price $0.08 each**

**China Tea Set**
15 pieces with handsome filigree design.
**Price: $0.75 each set**

 **Now, can you find six items that equal exactly $5.00?**

$3\frac{1}{2} + 8\frac{1}{6} + \frac{1}{8} = ?$ ✻ $\frac{1}{2} = \frac{2}{4} = \frac{4}{8}$ ✻ $0.5 = 0.50 = 0.500$ ✻ $123.45$

**Decimals: Addition & Subtraction**

# Running for the Gold

**Students will understand decimals on a concrete level by playing this simple game.**

## ⟲→ Directions

1. Duplicate the reproducible for each student.
2. Distribute the number cubes and reproducibles to the groups.
3. Ask group members to decide on the order of play.
4. Go over the rules of the game, as follows:

   a. A player rolls the number cubes. Example: 6, 2

   b. The player chooses the order of digits and writes the decimal in the Record Rolls column. Example: 0.62 is a better choice than 0.26.

   c. The player shades 62 boxes in MILE ONE to represent the decimal 0.62.

## ☆ Taking It Farther

This game can easily be converted to a decimal subtraction game. Students start with three shaded boxes and subtract with each roll. The student who "unshades" all the boxes wins.

## ✓ Assessing Skills

What strategies do students use for adding decimals—mentally grouping ones and tens, mentally rounding and working backward, or calculating with paper and pencil?

### LEARNING OBJECTIVE

Students add and subtract decimals.

### GROUPING

Cooperative groups

### MATERIALS

For each student:

✳ *Running for the Gold* reproducible (p. 56)

For each group:

✳ 2 number cubes labeled 1–6

# Running for the Gold

Roll the number cubes to make the greatest decimal you can. Record it in the table below, shade the boxes to represent the decimal, and you're off and running! The first player to mark off three miles is the winner.

| RECORD ROLLS | | Mile One | |
|---|---|---|---|
| 0.___ ___   0.___ ___ | | | |
| 0.___ ___   0.___ ___ | | | |
| 0.___ ___   0.___ ___ | | | |
| 0.___ ___   0.___ ___ | | | |
| 0.___ ___   0.___ ___ | | | |

| RECORD ROLLS | | Mile Two | |
|---|---|---|---|
| 0.___ ___   0.___ ___ | | | |
| 0.___ ___   0.___ ___ | | | |
| 0.___ ___   0.___ ___ | | | |
| 0.___ ___   0.___ ___ | | | |
| 0.___ ___   0.___ ___ | | | |

| RECORD ROLLS | | Mile Three | |
|---|---|---|---|
| 0.___ ___   0.___ ___ | | | |
| 0.___ ___   0.___ ___ | | | |
| 0.___ ___   0.___ ___ | | | |
| 0.___ ___   0.___ ___ | | | |
| 0.___ ___   0.___ ___ | | | |

# Decimal Points Everywhere

This crossword puzzle points students to success with the multiplication and division of decimals.

## ✏ Directions

1. Duplicate the *Decimal Points Everywhere* reproducible.

2. Review the multiplication of decimals as follows.

   **a.** Multiply as you would with whole numbers.

$$
\begin{array}{r}
8.2 \\
\times\ 1.3 \\
\hline
246 \\
82\phantom{6} \\
\hline
1066
\end{array}
$$

   **b.** Put as many decimal places in the product as there are in the factors combined.

$$
\begin{array}{rl}
8.2 & \leftarrow 1\ \text{place} \\
\times\ 1.3 & \leftarrow 1\ \text{place} \\
\hline
246 & \\
82\phantom{6} & \\
\hline
10.66 & \leftarrow 2\ \text{places}
\end{array}
$$

3. Review the division of decimals as follows.

   **a.** Place the decimal point in the quotient directly above decimal point in dividend.

$$7\overline{)6.23}$$

   **b.** Divide as you would with whole numbers.

$$
\begin{array}{r}
0.89 \\
7\overline{)6.23} \\
5\,6\phantom{3} \\
\hline
63 \\
63 \\
\hline
\end{array}
$$

4. Distribute the reproducible and allow students to complete it on their own. You may wish to let them use calculators.

## ★ Taking It Farther

Encourage students to make their own decimal puzzles for classmates to solve. Use the crossword squares on the reproducible and have students write their own problems. Require them to make a key for checking.

## ✓ Assessing Skills

❋ Are students counting decimal places from the left or the right?

❋ Encourage students to estimate to see that the answers are reasonable.

# Decimal Points Everywhere

Can you find the decimal point in each of these answers? This crossword puzzle is sure to sharpen your skills and point you toward success with multiplication and division of decimals.

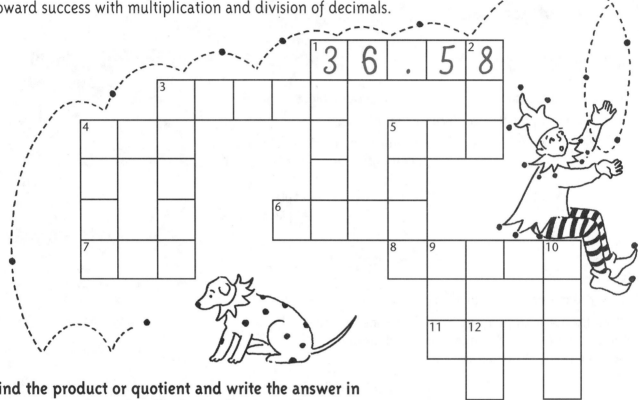

**Find the product or quotient and write the answer in the crossword puzzle. The decimal point will occupy a square. The first one has been done for you.**

## ACROSS

**1.** $5.9 \times 6.2 =$ _36.58_

**3.** $3.3 \times 3.8 =$ _____

**4.** $28.2 \div 6 =$ _____

**5.** $19.6 \div 2 =$ _____

**6.** $162.6 \div 6 =$ _____

**7.** $49.2 \div 6 =$ _____

**8.** $87.03 \div 3 =$ _____

**11.** $27.2 \div 2 =$ _____

## DOWN

**1.** $6.7 \times 5.1 =$ _____

**2.** $26.4 \div 3 =$ _____

**3.** $8.1 \times 2.2 =$ _____

**4.** $2.14 \times 2 =$ _____

**5.** $4.8 \times 1.9 =$ _____

**9.** $36.4 \div 4 =$ _____

**10.** $1.4 \times 1.2 =$ _____

**12.** $22.2 \div 6 =$ _____

$3\frac{1}{2} + 8\frac{1}{6} + \frac{1}{8} = ?$  ※  $\frac{1}{2} = \frac{2}{4} = \frac{4}{8}$  ※  $0.5 = 0.50 = 0.500$  ※  $123.45$

**Decimals: Multiplication & Division**

# Decimal Puzzlers

**Students use their favorite pictures to make decimal puzzles for classmates to solve.**

## Directions

1. Instruct students to select and cut out large color pictures from the magazines. Have them glue the pictures to the tagboard or paper.

2. When the glue has dried thoroughly, students trim the pictures into 6-inch by 8-inch rectangles. Then they cut the pictures into 2-inch by 2-inch puzzle squares. You may want to draw the puzzle diagram on the board for reference.

3. Tell students to write multiplication or division decimal problems on the back of each square. If possible, laminate the puzzle pieces so they will last longer.

4. To make the puzzle base, students draw 6-inch by 8-inch rectangles in the center of pieces of tagboard. Then they draw lines to divide the rectangles into 2-inch by 2-inch squares.

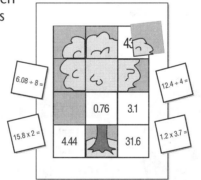

5. Tell students to assemble their puzzles on the base. Ask them to lift each piece and write the answer to the multiplication or division problem on the puzzle base below. When the puzzle is constructed, the pieces will be placed on the corresponding answers.

6. Have students place the puzzle pieces in zip plastic bags and attach to the puzzle bases with large paper clips.

7. Encourage students to trade decimal puzzles and let the fun begin!

## Taking It Farther

Make a bulletin board entitled "Decimal Puzzlers." Display several puzzles that have been put together. Post several other puzzles for students to work when they have available independent time.

## Assessing Skills

※ When multiplying decimals, do students count the decimal places in both factors before placing the decimal point in the product?

※ When dividing decimals, do students place the decimal point in the quotient directly above the decimal point in the dividend?

$3\frac{1}{2} + 8\frac{1}{6} + \frac{1}{8} = ?$ ✸ $\frac{1}{2} = \frac{2}{4} = \frac{4}{8}$ ✸ $0.5 = 0.50 = 0.500$ ✸ $123.456789 + 9876.54321 = ?$

# Do I Have Problems!

Here are a variety of fraction and decimal problems to pose to students. Use them as homework puzzles, as extra-credit brain teasers, or post them on a Problem of the Day bulletin board.

## WHO AM I?

**a.** I have four digits, and they are all odd.

**b.** The number in the hundredths place is 3.

**c.** The numbers in the hundredths place and ones place are equal.

**d.** The number in the tens place is the product of the numbers in the hundredths place and the ones place.

**e.** The number in the tenths place is greater than 4, and it is equal to one of the other digits. [93.93]

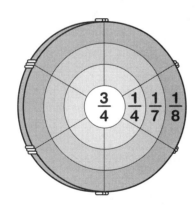

## DART THROWER

A dart thrower made exactly $3\frac{1}{7}$ points after throwing five darts. Where did the darts land? [Four darts landed on $\frac{3}{4}$ and one dart landed on $\frac{1}{7}$.]

## WHAT'S NEXT?

Complete the patterns.

$\frac{1}{2}$, 1, $1\frac{1}{2}$, 2, $2\frac{1}{2}$, _____, _____, _____, _____     [3, $3\frac{1}{2}$, 4, $4\frac{1}{2}$]

$\frac{3}{4}$, $1\frac{1}{4}$, $1\frac{3}{4}$, $2\frac{1}{4}$, $2\frac{3}{4}$, _____, _____, _____, _____     [$3\frac{1}{4}$, $3\frac{3}{4}$, $4\frac{1}{4}$, $4\frac{3}{4}$]

12, $11\frac{1}{4}$, $10\frac{1}{2}$, $9\frac{3}{4}$, 9, _____, _____, _____, _____     [$8\frac{1}{4}$, $7\frac{1}{2}$, $6\frac{3}{4}$, 6]

$\frac{1}{2}$, $1\frac{3}{4}$, 3, $4\frac{1}{4}$, $5\frac{1}{2}$, _____, _____, _____, _____     [$6\frac{3}{4}$, 8, $9\frac{1}{4}$, $10\frac{1}{2}$]

## MAGIC SQUARE

Combine the fractions in the adjacent cells to equal 1. Use each cell only once.

|  |  |  |
|---|---|---|
| $\frac{2}{3}$ | $\frac{1}{6}$ | $\frac{7}{10}$ |
| $\frac{1}{6}$ | $\frac{1}{5}$ | $\frac{1}{10}$ |
| $\frac{1}{7}$ | $\frac{3}{7}$ | $\frac{3}{7}$ |

You may not use cells like this:

|  |  |  |
|---|---|---|
| $\frac{2}{3}$ | $\frac{1}{6}$ | $\frac{7}{10}$ |
| $\frac{1}{6}$ | $\frac{1}{5}$ | $\frac{1}{10}$ |
| $\frac{1}{7}$ | $\frac{3}{7}$ | $\frac{3}{7}$ |

You may use cells like this:

|  |  |  |
|---|---|---|
| $\frac{2}{3}$ | $\frac{1}{6}$ | $\frac{7}{10}$ |
| $\frac{1}{6}$ | $\frac{1}{5}$ | $\frac{1}{10}$ |
| $\frac{1}{7}$ | $\frac{3}{7}$ | $\frac{3}{7}$ |

$[\frac{1}{6} + \frac{1}{6} + \frac{2}{3}; \frac{7}{10} + \frac{1}{10} + \frac{1}{5}; \frac{1}{7} + \frac{3}{7} + \frac{3}{7}]$

## MOVING DAY

The teacher was packing her books in boxes at the end of the school year. One-half of the books went in a large box on top of her desk. One-fourth of the books went into two small boxes in her cabinet. Twelve of the books were put into drawers, 15 of the books were given away to the students, and the other 3 were taken home for the summer. How many books did she have in all? [120 books]

## PIGGY BANK TROUBLES

Steven wanted $0.25 to put into a gum ball machine. He emptied coins from his piggy bank on the bed and discovered that he didn't have any quarters. If he added his eight coins together, he had enough change to make exactly $0.25. How many pennies, nickels, and dimes did he have? [1 dime, 2 nickels, 5 pennies]

## GARDENING FUN

Cecil, Patrick, and Amos were planting a garden at school and wanted to share expenses. Cecil spent $13.00 on fertilizers and soil mix, and Patrick spent $15.00 on plants and seeds. Amos bought a shovel for $11.00. Who paid exactly one-third the total amount? Who paid less than one-third and by how much? Who paid more than one-third and by how much? [Cecil paid exactly one-third. Amos paid less by $2.00. Patrick paid more by $2.00.]

# MYSTERY NUMBERS

Shade the numbers described in the questions below.

| 21 | 15 | 100 | 9 | 16 | 30 | 8 |
|----|----|-----|---|----|----|---|

How many thirds are in 3? [9]

How many thirds are in 5? [15]

How many thirds are in 7? [21]

How many fourths are in 2? [8]

How many fourths are in 4? [16]

How many fifths are in 6? [30]

What mystery number remains? _____ [100]

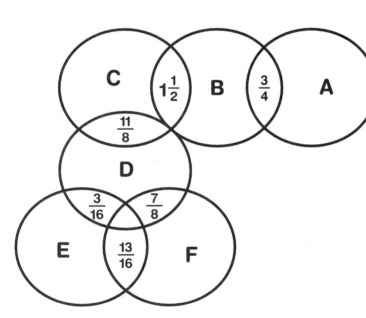

# CIRCLE MATH

Where some circles overlap, there is a number. This number is the sum of the value of the two circles. Each circle has one of these fraction values: $\frac{5}{4}$, $\frac{1}{4}$, $\frac{1}{2}$, $\frac{1}{8}$, $\frac{3}{4}$, and $\frac{1}{16}$. No two circles have the same number. Can you find the fraction value for each circle?
[A = $\frac{1}{2}$, B = $\frac{1}{4}$, C = $\frac{5}{4}$, D = $\frac{1}{8}$, E = $\frac{1}{16}$, F = $\frac{3}{4}$]

# LETTER ADDITION

Each letter stands for a number from 0 to 9, but no two letters have the same number. Find the number expressed by each letter. (Hint: X = 2, R = 7, and P = 9)

```
    P T.MX K
 +  O L.T X Z
   M R O.V V Z
```

[P = 9, T = 3, M = 1, X = 2, K = 0, O = 8, L = 5, Z = 6,
R = 7, V = 4; 93.120 + 85.326 = 178.446]

# In My Opinion

The activity _____ was:

| | | | | | | | | | |
|---|---|---|---|---|---|---|---|---|---|

Easy                                                                                    Hard

because:

_____

_____

_____

_____

My work on this activity was:

| | | | | | | |
|---|---|---|---|---|---|---|

poor                        fair                        good                        excellent

because:

_____

_____

_____

I used the following math strategy or strategies:

➤ _____        ➤ _____

➤ _____        ➤ _____

➤ _____        ➤ _____

I would share this tip with someone who is about to do this activity:

_____

_____

_____

# ⟳ Activity _____ Date _____

## TEACHER ASSESSMENT FORM

| Student | | | | | |
|---|---|---|---|---|---|
| **UNDERSTANDING** | | | | | |
| Identifies the problem or task. | | | | | |
| Understands the math concept. | | | | | |
| **SOLVING** | | | | | |
| Develops and carries out a plan. | | | | | |
| Uses strategies, models, and tools effectively. | | | | | |
| **DECIDING** | | | | | |
| Is able to convey reasoning behind decision making. | | | | | |
| Understands why approach did or didn't work. | | | | | |
| **LEARNING** | | | | | |
| Comments on solution. | | | | | |
| Connects solution to other math or real-world applications. | | | | | |
| Makes general rule about solution or extends it to a more complicated problem. | | | | | |
| **COMMUNICATING** | | | | | |
| Understands and uses mathematical language effectively. | | | | | |
| **COLLABORATING** | | | | | |
| Participates by sharing ideas with partner or group members. | | | | | |
| Listens to partner or other group members. | | | | | |
| **ACCOMPLISHING** | | | | | |
| Shows progress in problem solving. | | | | | |
| Undertakes difficult tasks and perseveres in solving them. | | | | | |
| Is confident of mathematical abilities. | | | | | |

## SCORING RUBRIC

| 3 | 2 | 1 |
|---|---|---|
| Fully accomplishes the task. Shows full understanding of key mathematical idea(s). Communicates thinking clearly using oral explanation or written, symbolic, or visual means. | Partially accomplishes the task. Shows partial understanding of key mathematical idea(s). Oral or written explanation partially communicates thinking but may be incomplete, misdirected, or not clearly presented. | Does not accomplish the task. Shows little or no grasp of key mathematical idea(s). Recorded work or oral explanation is fragmented and not understandable. |

*Decimals and Fractions* Scholastic Professional Books